A Collection of Miscellaneous Essays / by T. Mozeen

LIST of SUBSCRIBERS.

Mr. Thorold.
Thurkhill.
Troughton.
Dr. Thomas.

V.

James Varnier, *Esq*;
Mr. R. Vincent, *jun.*
Vernon.

W.

Mr. Wallis.
J. Williamson.
T. Williamson.
Robert Williams.
Wefton.
Thomas Walker.
Wm. Williams.
John Williams.
Robert Walfh, *Esq*;
Mr. John Weftwood.

Mr. Winter.
Ward.
White.
Charles White.
John Walker.
John Williams.
Brafield Williams.
Thomas Williams.
Wetherall.
Wood.
Weft.
Woodifield.
Watfon.
Mrs. Walker.

Y.

Mr. Yates
Mrs. Yates.
Mr. Young.
Thomas Yewd.
Wm. Yewd.

A

Lucy *of the Village*, &c.

The Music by Mr. *Patterfall.*

Sung by Mr. *Mattocks.*

1759.

I.

AGAIN the blooming Month of *May*
   Calls the Swains to sport and play;
While wanton Birds, on every Spray,
   Stretch their Throats to praise the Day:
And *Lucy* of the Village Queen,
Smiling trips it o'er the Green.

II.

But Nymph, without Exception Fair,
  What mean those Flowrets in thy Hair?
O lovely Child of Nature's Care,
  Who stript for Thee the Graces bare,
Such trivial Ornaments displace,
  What Flower can add to *Lucy*'s Face?

III.

III.

No threatning Clouds, no lowering Skies,
  Are e'er beheld in *Lucy*'s Eyes :
Nor can her Bofom Spleen devife,
  In that foft Bed, good Humour lies ;
And all muft own the Truths I tell,
  Whoever faw my charming Belle.

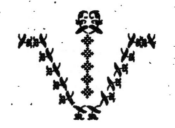

The

The Recluse.

Sung by Mr. *Mattocks.*

I.

A T Eve with the Woodlark I reft,
    I rife on each Morn with the fame;
By the Note of the Nightingale bleft,
    I laugh at the Trumpet of Fame.

II.

My Meals without Riches are crown'd,
    Fair Temperance comes in their Stead;
At my Table, tho' Plenty be found,
    Exceffes fhall never be bred.

III.

From the Top of my Primrofy Hill,
    How many proud Buildings I fee!
The Lords of them, envy who will;
    My Eafe and my Cottage for me.

IV.

IV.

I labour, but leave when I pleafe ;
  I ftudy,——but not to my Hurt ;
Revere my great Maker's Decrees,
  And avoid all political Dirt.

V.

I fmile at my Country's Increafe
  In Commerce, Religion and Arms :
My Heart and my Hand are for thefe ;
  A *Briton*, whom Liberty warms.

VI.

No Mortal one Penny I owe,
  I ftick to each fcriptural Text ;
Wou'd all in this World but live fo,
  How fearlefs they'd go to the next.

A New

A *New* EPILOGUE,

Spoke by Miss *Pitt*, in the Character of one of the Boys of the School on *St. Augustine's Back, Bristol*; endowed by the late charitable *Edward Colston*, Efq;

Avours too oft at random Fortune pours;
F Now fwells the Cheats, anon the Mifer's Stores;
Now rules the Horfe-match, — now prefides at
    Drums,
And moft reforts where Reafon feldom comes.
t was not fo of old —— or Sages ly'd;
Fortune and Truth once journey'd Side by Side; }
'erhaps they parted when our *Colfton* dy'd!
And now in fad Defpair a Son to find
His Like, among the Race of human Kind,
Chance wildly wanders; torturing wretched Elves,
And keeps us ftill at Variance with ourfelves.
s there a Way the Goddefs to regain,
Or muft our Labour, Labour be in vain?
Methinks our honour'd Founder, from the Skies,
A Way there is, my gentle Child, replies;
urfue thofe Tracts I ftudy'd for your School,
ngraft your Heart with each digefted Rule,
'ill Time's all ripening Hand fhall bring you forth,
To grace my Memory, and affert your Worth.
       Then,

Then, in whatever Sphere you're doom'd to live,
Be pious, modeft :———diligently ftrive
To gain good Men ; ———remember, not defert,
But public Love firft led thee where thou art.
Avoid the Proud, the Coxcomb, and the Fool,
The common Buts of grinning Ridicule.
The Wanton's well diffembled Lures deteft,
That Bane of Youth, that univerfal Peft.
The Idler fcorn ;———fome Bufinefs always find ;
Abhor a Lie,———worft Meannefs of the Mind.
But little fpeak,———and be that little right,
For Folly's Phrafes Wifdom's Ears affright.
Be true to Truft, to friendly Acts incline,
So fhalt thou live a much-lov'd Son of mine,
Avoid the Bad,———and fix good Fortune thine.

Time took by the Forelock, at Kilternan, *the Seat of* John Adair, *Esq; in the County of* Dublin.

I.

Dislike not my Song, though 'tis to an old Tune,
No melting *Italian,* or *French* Rigadoon;
The *French* are made 'up with Intrigue and
          Defign,
And pleafe me in Nought but their Abfence and Wine.
                              Derry down, &c.

II.

With Ruin fatigu'd, and grown quite melancholic,
I'll fing you how old Daddy Time took a Frolic,
By the Help of good Claret, to diffipate Cares;
The Spot was *Kilternan,* the Houfe was *Adair's*.
                              Derry down, &c.

III.

Not us'd to the Sight of the foberer Race,
With the Door in her Hand, the Maid laugh'd in his Face
For fhe thought by his Figure he might be at beft,
Some plodding Mechanic, or Prig of a Prieft.
                              Derry down, &c.

IV.

But foon as he faid that he came for a Glafs,
Without farther Referve fhe reply'd he might pafs:
Yet fmoak'd his bald Pate, as he totter'd along,
And defpis'd him, as Moderns defpife an old Song.
Derry down, &c.

V.

Jack Adair was at Table, with Six of his Friends,
Who for making him Drunk, he was making Amends:
Time hop'd at his Prefence none there were affronted;
Sit down Boy, fays *Jack*, and prepare to be hunted.
Derry down, &c.

VI.

They drank Hand to Fift for Six Bottles and more,
Till down tumbled Time, and began for to fnore;
Five Gallons of Claret they pour'd on his Head,
And were going to take the old Soaker to Bed.
Derry down, &c.

VII.

But *Jack*, who's poffefs'd of a pretty Eftate,
And wou'd to the Lord it was ten times as great,
Thought aptly enough, that if Time didn't wake,
He might lofe all he had, by the World's running back.
Derry down, &c.

VIII.

VIII.

So twitching his Forelock, Time open'd his Eyes,
And ſtaggering, ſtar'd, with a deal of Surprize;
Quoth he, I muſt mow down Ten Millions of Men,
But e'er you drink thrice, I'll be with you again.
Derry down, &c.

IX.

For your Claret, my Boy, give me hold of your Fiſt;
Thou'rt as honeſt a Fellow as ever yet p—ſt.
Go on with your Bumpers, your Beef, and good Cheer,
And the Darling of Time ſhall be *Johnny Adair*.

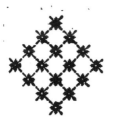

An

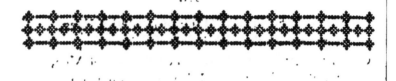

An EPILOGUE,

Spoke by Mrs. *Green*, at the Theatre, *Briftol*, after the Play of the *Confcious Lovers*; acted for the Benefit of the *Briftol Infirmary*.

MAN cannot change fevere Decrees of Fate,
But bleft the Hand, that ftrives to mitigate;
The truly wife,————the charitable Heart,
    That deigns its Store fo freely to impart,
Erects a Bafe no Envy can annoy,
No Malice fhake, nor Time itfelf deftroy.
With Eyes enraptur'd, Bofoms fraught with Glee,
We own thy Power, O heaven-born Charity!
Dejected Minds, with Ails and Anguifh torn,
Thus to relieve, thus comfort the Forlorn;
Nature's great Sire approves; fuch Odours rife
Superior to the pompous Sacrifice;
Adorn the mortal State, and waft ye to the Skies.

A BAL-

A BALLAD.

Set by Mr. *Patterfall*.

I.

WHAT now ferve foft Beds of gay Flowers to
me ?
What now ferve the Plains, once productive of
Glee !
Why fhines the bright Sun on a Wretch, but alas !
To recall to *Alexis*, how happy he was ?
Each Violet I fmell to, fays, Such was her Breath ;
Each Step thro' the Glen's, a Step nearer to Death ;
Since *Phœbus*, who witnefs'd our Tendernefs there,
Tells the wondering World, fhe's as falfe as fhe's fair.

II.

When Ev'ning to rooft on the Beech brings the Dove,
I figh, and look up,———fuch our Leffons of Love ;
The Tear trickles then ; and my Dog feems to fay,
Whence happens this Change?———Ar't offended with
Tray ?
Not fo, my poor Faithful, my well-belov'd Brute,
Such Crimes as I mourn for, with thee do not fuit ;
Tho' I chide thee, thou lov'ft me ; I am ever thy Care ;
So *Polly* once faid,———but fhe's falfe as fhe's fair.

III.

III.

Fellow Swains be advis'd, nor the Knee to her bend,
Who is not her own, can be no Shepherd's Friend;
Tho' true she be blest with each personal Grace,
As hateful her Manners, as lovely her Face;
From an Angel-like Form, who such Harm cou'd suppose,
Her Heart's a foul Canker, that preys on a Rose;
Like *Syren* she'll sing ye to Rocks and Despair,
But despise her, as I do;————she's false as she's fair.

The BEDLAMITE.

I.

TIS not on the Face difplay'd,
  What I fuffer, cruel Maid!
  A burning Poifon lurks unfeen :
   O eafe me; eafe my fad Chagrin!
See thro' yon fiery Lake, yon flaming Flood,
Fierce Dragons come to drink my Blood.
   Why *Jove* doft thou thus fet them on ?
   O what have I done,
   My dear, dear, dazling Sun,
    That no Wind from the Sea
    Blows Tidings to me,
   Whilft the Tyrant frowns on my Throne ?

II.

Shall we to the Meadows go,
  Where the Butter-flowers blow,
And the dainty Daizies grow ?
    I fay No, no, no, no, no, no.

C   For

For lend me a while your Ear;
How can I be merry,
Whilſt you guzzle Sherry,
And I muſt ſip Small Beer?———

III.

Give me the Reward,
Give me the Reward;
And fill the Goblet high:
I now the Traitor ſpy;———
Tread ſoft and fair,
All light as Air,
'Tis my Belief,
Yon Plantane Leaf,
Conceals him from your Eye.

IV.

'Tis a *Spaniard* on my Life!———
Tawny Face,———bloody Knife!———
But let the Bells merrily ring;
We have Store of great Guns,
And fine *Chelſea* Buns,
And the *Burgundy* runs;
And we love, and we honour the King.

V.

Nay be not ſo harſh with your Smiles;
Your Frowns are more pleaſant to me.
Hark! hearken to Puſs on the Tiles!———
She's juſt ſuch a Lady as thee.

VI.

VI.

Ah *Fanny!* Why doſt thou ſo ſadly complain?
Thou can'ſt not ſure envy my temperate Brain.
  Off, off the Courſe,
  That damn'd trotting Horſe:
  I'll hold Six to Four
  You hear on't no more;
For *Pruſſia* has beat them again.————

VII.

Of Reaſon I held a Leaſe,
But long, very long 't has been out:
 O Landlord, renew, if you pleaſe!
Help Counſellor,————bring it about.
 What!————Nothing without your Fees?————
Ah tickle me not for a Trout.————

VIII.

  How now, ſaucy *Jack*;
  Why appear'ſt thou in Black?————
A Packet to me ſay'ſt directed;
  Ha! ha! ha! ha!
  Bow Enemies, bow!
  Or I'll harraſs you now:
'Tis the Comet ſo long we've expected.————

IX.

IX.

Nay, footh me not; for well I know,
To cure my tortur'd Heart of Woe,
 Is not to Mortal given :
She only can my Senfe reftore,
Who robb'd me of it once before;
 An Angel, now in Heaven.

The

The TUTOR.

A BALLAD.

Sung by *Andrews*, at *Sadlers Wells*.

I.

WHEN *Jenny* the gay I firſt courted to wed,
　　Whole Reams I of Love to her ſent;
But back ſhe return'd them, and ſcornfully ſaid,
　　That ſhe cou'dn't tell what the Fool meant.

II.

Reſolv'd not to give up the Matter ſo tame,
　　I follow'd wherever ſhe went;
At the Park,—at the Play,—at the Route 'twas the ſame;
　　Still ſhe cou'dn't tell what the Fool meant.———

III.

Her Maid was my Friend; and advis'd me to hope;
　　Or elſe I had quitted the Scent;
For my Tale ſhe wou'd ſtop, if my Lips I did ope,
　　With———She cou'dn't tell what the Fool meant.

C 3　　　　　　　　　　　IV.

IV.

But *Molly*, in lieu of a Handful of Gold,
  In the Chamber of *Jenny* me pent;
Three long Hours and more I lay ſhiv'ring with Cold,
  That the Girl might know what the Fool meant.—

V.

But what are three Hours, nay Threſcore and Three,
  To be crown'd at the laſt with Content;——
Young *Jenny*'s no longer hard-hearted to me,
  Since I ſhew'd her what 'twas the Fool meant.

A Welcome

A Welcome Home to the brave General
CLIVE.

A BALLAD.

RECITATIVE.

FROM barbarous Climes, and Nations far re-
mote,
  O'er Sands, and Rocks, and Seas fhe's wing'd
  her Way;
Fair Fame behold, with Afpect heavenly bright;
And in her Hand fhe brings our Eaftern Chief!

AIR.

When *Clive* is repeated, what Bofom but warms,
Who, whilft yet but a Youth, gave all *Afia* Alarms.
Who, to court rough Encounters, ftept out of his Way;
Obtain'd a Command, but rejected the Pay.
 Such noble Examples, ye *Britons*, purfue;
 And welcome to *Britain*, a *Briton* like you.

II.

His Orders ſcarce ta'en e'er he *Arkat* ſubdu'd ;
Yet ſuffer'd no pillaging, cruel and rude :——
The Poor he protected ; the Province he ſpar'd ;
But ſhov'd back with Scorn the ſparkling Reward.
   The noble Example ye *Britons* purſue ;
   For *Clive* is a *Briton*, a *Briton* like you.

III.

Some few Forts reduc'd on *Arani*'s wide Plains,
The Foe he eſpies, but their Number diſdains ;——
An obſtinate Action five Hours was held,
When a total Defeat gave to *Clive* the red Field.
   An Action as noble, as gallant as true,
   And *Britons* 'twas done by a *Briton* like you.

IV.

At *Kaveri Pakam* he forc'd them retire ;
(The *Frenchmen* can never ſtand long *Britiſh* Fire)
With thoſe he took Priſoners, and thoſe were o'erthrown,
An Army he beat twice as large as his own.
   With Acts many more, wiſe, firm, gallant and true ;
   Then welcome to *Briton*, a *Briton* like you.

The

The Lover's Resolve.

A BALLAD.

I.

THE Nymph that I love is a dangerous Fair;
 Her Eyes dart so fiercely; her Breasts do so
   heave;
 Whenever I speak, she's so cross, I declare;
 I do nought all the Day but torment me, and
  · grieve.——
  But if once I shou'd get,
  My fair one, my *Bett*,
To yonder's green Arbor, surrounded with Sweets;
  Where Violet and Primrose,
  And Woodbine there too grows;
Let her frown as she will,———I'll feel how her Heart
 beats.

II.

II.

If gently fhe take it, I'll ply her more clofe :——
 Young Cupid, play round, and excite her to Love ;—
Shou'd fhe tafte kind my Vow, I'll double the Dofe,
 And prefs her of Joys the fublimeft to prove.——
   For the Slight and the Pain,
   That I late did fuftain,
I feek from the Wanton an ample Return ;
   No Time to be cruel,
   I'll give my dear Jewel ;
But lay on thy Altar the Maid 'till fhe burn.

The *Militia-Man*.

A BALLAD.

Sung at *Sadlers Wells*.

BY our Conduct Abroad, and our Councils at
        Home,
  We've so cow'd the poor *French*, and so humbled
      proud *Rome*,
That they dare n't look up : why let's keep 'em still down,
For the Honour of *Britain*,—the Right of the Crown.
      They are rascally Foes ;
      Then, O follow them close ;
      And second the Blow,
      That lately you know,
Was dealt them by *Prussia*, that Son of Renown :
      Their dastardly Bands,
      Shrink under our Hands ;
To no gallant Deed can their Armies be stirr'd :
      Triumphant then sing,
      And make the Air ring,
      With bless, bless the King !
Our Guardian!——our Father !——our Friend *George* the
      Third !

II.

II.

We are *Britons* free born, and as such let's behave,
With Hearts, Hands, and Purses, 'gainst Fool, Tool, and
     Knave.
O Pope! O Pretender! O Monarch of *France*!
Where, where are you now? Are ye sick of the Dance?
     In our Sovereign's Right,
     We prepare for the Fight,
     E'er our Liberties fall,
     Be Militia-Men all.
Turn our Plough-shares to Swords, and to meet ye advance.
     Sound Trumpet! Beat Drum!————
     Come, *Frenchmen!* Come! Come;————
Yet hear from a Foe the Advice of a Word;
     Starv'd Scoundrels beware,
     For your Souls have a Care;
     He dies, who first dare
Set a Foot on the Bounds of great King *George* the Third.

Amyntor

Amyntor *and* Solon.

A CANTATA.

RECITATIVE.

WITH Eye fevere, and four contracted Brow,
The gay *Amyntor*, rigid *Solon* fought;
Him found fupinely ftretcht on rofeate Bed,
And thus the enamour'd Indolent befpoke.----

AIR.

Deaf to Honour, deaf to Fame,
To thy great Forefather's Name;
He whofe Counfels *Britain* fteer'd,
He whofe Valour *Belgia* fear'd;
Fond Love, and its inglorious Charms,
Quit thee! nor flight a World in Arms.

RECIT.

A confcious Sigh, *Amyntor*'s Bofom heav'd;
Shame for a While, the Flow of Utterance ftopt:
The Conflict paft, his drooping Eye-lids rear'd,
In Tone fubmiffive, he the Sage addreft.

AIR.

Air.

Thy wholefome Dictates I obey;
  For ever juft, and good; -
To ferve my King I'll ftrait away,
  And rifque my vital Blood.
Yes, *Lucy*,——deareft Maid, I go;
  Excufe the fond Adieu.————
Since, fhou'd I fee,————too well I know,
  How hard to part from you.

A fea-

A *sea-faring* BALLAD.

Introduced by Mr. *Beard,* in the Character of a
Sailor, at the laſt Revival of the Comedy of *The
Fair Quaker of Deal,* at *Drury-Lane* Theatre ;
accompanied by the Boat's Crew.

I.

HOW little do the Landmen know
 Of what we Sailors feel ;
 When Waves do mount, and Winds do blow :
  But we have Hearts of Steel.
No Danger can affright us,
 No Enemy ſhall flout ;
We'll make the Monſieurs right us ;
 So————tofs the Can about.

GRAND CHORUS.

No Danger can affright us, &c.

II.

II.

Stick ftout to Orders Mefs-mates ;
   We'll plunder, burn and fink ;
Then *France* have at your firft Rates ;
   For *Britons* never fhrink.
We'll rummage all we fancy,
   And bring them in by Scores ;
And *Moll,* and *Kate,* and *Nancy,*
   Shall roll in Louis d'Qrs.

III.

While here at *Deal* we lie, Boys,
   With our noble Commodore,
We'll fpend our Wages freely, Boys ;
   And then to Sea for more.————
In Peace, we'll drink, and fing, Boys,
   In War we'll never fly ;————
Here's a Health to *George* our King, Boys,
   And the royal Family.

A Defcription of a Fox-Chafe,

That happened in the County of *Dublin*, 1744, with the Earl of *Meath*'s Hounds.

A B A L L A D.

Tune, *Shelah Nagirah.*

I.

HARK, hark, jolly Sportfmen, a while to a Tale, Which, to pay your Attention, I hope, will not fail :
'Tis of Lads, and of Horfes, and Dogs, that ne'er tire
O'er Stone Walls, and Hedges, thro' Dale, Bog and Briar :
A Pack of fuch Hounds, and a Set of fuch Men,
'Tis a fhrewd Chance if ever ye meet with again.
Had *Nimrod*, the mightieft of Hunters, been there,
'Fore gad he had fhook like an Afpen for Fear.
La, la, la, &c.

II.

II.

In Seventeen Hundred and Forty and Four,
The Fifth of *December* ———— I think 'twas no more;
At Five in the Morning, by moſt of the Clocks,
We rode from *Kilruddery*, to try for a Fox;————
The *Laughlin*'s Town Landlord, the bold *Owen Bray*,
With 'Squire *Adair*, ſure were with us that Day;
Joe Debill, Hal Preſton, that Huntſman ſo ſtout,
Dick Holmes (a few others); and ſo we ſet out.
La, la, la, &c.

III.

We had caſt off the Hounds for an Hour or more,
When *Wanton* ſet up a moſt tuneable Roar:
Hark to *Wanton !* cry'd *Joe*————and the reſt were not ſlack,
* For *Wanton*'s no Trifler eſteem'd by the Pack:
* Old *Bonny* and *Collier* came readily in ;
And every Dog join'd in the muſical Din.
Had *Diana* been there, ſhe'd been pleas'd to the Life,
And ſome of the Lads got a goddeſs to Wife.————
La, la, la, &c.

---

* Favourite Hounds of Lord *Meath*'s.

IV.

IV.

Ten Minutes paſt Nine was the Time o'the Day,
When *Reynard* unkennell'd, and this was his Play ;
As ſtrong from *Killeagar*, as tho' he cou'd fear none ;
Away he bruſh'd round by the Houſe at *Kilternan* ;
To *Carrick Mines* thence, and to *Cherrywood* then ;
Steep *Shank Hill* he climb'd, and to *Ballyman Glenn.*
Bray Common he paſt ; leap'd Lord *Angleaſed's* Wall ;
And ſeem'd to ſay, Little I value you all.
        La, la, la, &c.

V.

He run Buſhes, Groves, up to *Carbury Boarns* ;
Joe Debill, and *Preſton,* kept leading by Turns ;
The Earth it was open,——but *Reynard* was ſtout ;
Tho' he cou'd have got in, yet he choſe to keep out :
To *Malpaſs's* Summits away then he flew ;
At *Dalkey's* Stone Common, we had him in View.
He ſhot on thro' *Bullock* to *Shrub Glenagary* ;
And ſo on to *Mount Town,* where *Larry* grew weary.
        La, la, la, &c.

VI.

Thro' *Roche's* Town Wood, like an Arrow he paſt,
And came to the ſteep Hills of *Dalkey* at laſt ;
There gallantly plung'd himſelf into the Sea,
And ſaid in his Heart, Sure none dare follow me.
But ſoon, to his Coſt, he perceiv'd that no Bounds
Cou'd ſtop the Purſuit of the ſtaunch mettl'd Hounds.
His Policy here didn't ſerve him a Ruſh :
Five Couple of Tartars were hard at his Bruſh.
        La, la, la, &c.

VII.

To recover the Shore, then again was his Drift:
But e're he cou'd reach to the Top of the Clift,
He found both of Speed and of Cunning a Lack;
Being way-laid, and kill'd by the reft of the Pack.
At his Death there were prefent the Lads that I've fung,
Save *Larry*, who, riding a Garron, was flung.
Thus ended, at length, a moft delicate Chace,
That held us five Hours and ten Minutes Space.

La, la, la, &c.

VIII.

We return'd to *Kilruddery*'s plentiful Board,
Where dwells Hofpitality, Truth, and my Lord ———
We talk'd o'er the Chace, and we toafted the Health
Of the Man who ne'er vary'd for Places or Wealth.
Owen Bray baulk'd a Leap; faid *Hal Prefton*,—'twas odd;
'Twas fhameful, cry'd *Jack*——by the great living G—d!
Said *Prefton*, I halloo'd, Get on, tho' you fall;
Or I'll leap over you, your blind Gelding and all.

La, la, la, &c.

IX.

Each Glafs was adapted to Freedom and Sport;
But party Affairs we confign'd to the Court.
Thus we finifh'd the reft of the Day, and the Night,
In gay flowing Bumpers, and focial Delight.
Then till the next Meeting, bid Farewel each Brother;
For fome they went one Way, and fome went another.
And as *Phœbus* befriended our earlier Roam,
So *Luna* took Care in conducting us Home.

La, la, la, &c.

An Æ N I G M A *solv'd.*

WHAT Things moſt hurt, yet leaſt diſpleaſe ;
    Who tells, obtains a Prize :
Then give it me ;————I'll do't with Eaſe ;
    My lovely *Lucy*'s Eyes.

On

On *seeing a young Lady play with a*
BUTTERFLY.

WHAT pretty Insect view with Care;
  And then inform me true,
 If in your Frame there's ought more rare
  Than in its gilded Hue?

Each Wing, with various Colours fraught,
 Ah, how divinely bright!———
And yet how soon, alas, when caught,
 They vanish from the Sight.———

No more (the beauteous Tints once gone)
 The Butterfly we prize;
But, from each Hand neglected thrown,
 Th' unpity'd Reptile dies.

Take heed, Miss *Nanny*, left your Case
 Too near resemble this:
Be not too fond of that fair Face,
 Nor check the proffer'd Bliss.———

You'll

You'll find your now all-powerful Charms,
   By Length of Time decay'd ;——
In vain you'll then unfold your Arms,
   All fly a poor old Maid.

To

_To_ L A U R A.

LD and coarfe, yet ftill a Rover ;
  Prone to change ; fantaftic Dame !——
In thy Thought, why lives the Lover ?
  Wrinkl'd Madam——fie, for Shame ! ——

At Fifteen Years the blooming Maid,
 With every Glance a Swain difarms :
But cool'd by Threefcore. Summers Shade,
 'Tis Time to lay down ufelefs Arms.

Then fling your Wafh and Paint afide ;
 You never more can Man controul.——
Go, fay your Pray'rs, difcard your Pride ;
 And cheat the D——l of a Soul.

A SONG.

Lternately, my Day and Night,
   In *Harriot*'s Face I fee——
By ten times than the Sun more bright,
   Whenever we agree.——

Her dimpl'd Cheeks, her faithlefs Breaft,
   All Nature's Pride outvie ;
The Rofe, and Pink, their Shame confeft ;
   At her Appearance die.——

Calm and ferene, her Looks appear ;
   And charm'd——the Swains obey ;
But ah, alas ! there's Danger near :
   Avoid ye Swains her Way !——

Ruffl'd, fhe knows no Reafon why
   The quick reverted Scene,
Shifts to a gloomy low'ring Sky,
   Of Horrors, and Chagreen.——

Her

Her Eyes, with fiery Paſſion red,
　Their wonted Softneſs loſe;
Far from her Brow is Sweetneſs fled,
　And from her Cheek, the Roſe.

Shepherds, Companions of my Youth,
　Avoid a Nymph ſo gay;————
And think upon this certain Truth,
　That Night ſucceeds the Day.————

EPIGRAM.

IN *Chloe*'s Abfence I'm' at Eafe;
   Her Prefence gives me Pain.————
Grant me, great Jove, 'mongft your Decrees,
   Never to fee her Face again.

ANOTHER,

On a young Lady's being angry that fhe was difco-
vered as fhe was cutting a Corn.

DEAR Mifs, you needn't thus have put
   Yourfelf into fo vile a Paffion :
What faw I, pray, except your Foot ?————
   And that by Chance,————not Inclination.——

On

On CONTENT.

An EPIGRAM.

I T is not Youth can give Content,
  Nor is it Wealth can fee;
  It is a Dower from Heaven fent,
   Tho' not to thee, or me.

It is not in the Monarch's Crown,
  Tho' he'd give Millions for't;
It dwells not in his Lordfhip's Frown,
  Or waits on him to Court.

It is not in a Coach and Six;
  It is not in a Garter;
'Tis not in Love or Politics,
  But 'tis in *Hodge* the Carter.

The FAGGOT.

A FABLE from Æ*fop*.

HE who neglects Advice from hoary Head,
Deferves whate'er ill Fortune may fucceed ;
For none the Paths of Joy, or Grief can fhew,
'Till found Experience teach them firft to know.
  Roger, a Hind, who fix-and-fifty Years
Had view'd the World, and buftl'd thro' its Cares ;
Seen Knavery profper, Honefty degraded ;
Vice ever brilliant, Virtue ever fhaded :————
That Gold cou'd only furnifh Wit, and Grace,
Senfe, Beauty, Merit, Modefty and Place ;
Retir'd for Life, unto his little Farm ;
There dwelt fecure from Envy, and from Harm :————
Yet meagre Sicknefs found out his Abode ;
(In vain Secretion from the Hand of God.)
His Wife and Children all around him preft ;
The Pillow rais'd, he thus the Boys addrefs'd ;————
  Weep not, my Sons, that I expiring lie ;
Now we exift ;————To-morrow, and we die.————
But weep, ye that are yet conftrain'd to live,
And thro' a dangerous World with Hardfhip ftrive.
Ye now are healthy, ftrong, and all together :
Heaven keep you fo ;—reach me that Faggot hither ;—
Take each a Stick, and let me fee ye break it ;——
Nothing more eafy ;—that other yonder—take it !————

Try

Try at it as 'tis bound ;—'twill never do ;———
The Moral's eafy ;— *Thomas*, what think you ?———
Search round the Globe, you'll find you never can
Fix on a Beaft fo mercilefs as Man.———
For Brutes at leaft on different Species prey,
But Men more favage, more of Brutes than they,
Practife all Arts each other to betray.———
If fever'd in your Principles you fteer,
Think on each fingle Stick, and juftly fear :
But as the Faggot with the Withy bound,
So if Accordance in your Wills be found,
If ftrictly join'd you lean to Reafon's Side,
Oppofe Oppreffion, Folly, Art and Pride,
Who fhall your Conduct, or your Thoughts difjoint ?
Firm Unanimity gains every Point.

EPIGRAM,

On a certain Congregation.

F all are d——n'd who at their Prayers
   Mind little what they fay ;
(Intent on fublunary Cares),
   Or whifper, laugh and play :

If Men are doom'd to heavy Curfe
   For gazing on the Fair ;
Or (what, alas ! is ten times worfe)
   The Ladies may not ftare ;

If Piety will not allow
   Of *Cupid*'s gentle Dartings ;
O my good G—d, I pray thee now,
   Have Mercy on *St. M*———'s.

A SONG.

A SONG.

T H E Truant-Boy, I own, I lov'd ;
 My Conduct ceafe to blame ;——
For had he woo'd with equal Fire,
 Each Nymph had done the fame.——

His Tongue wou'd melt the hardeft Heart ;
 His Eyes the chafteft She :
No wonder in the Conqueft then,
 Obtain'd o'er filly me.——

A courtly Dame cou'd fcarce withftand
 His foft beguiling Tale ;
Ah! how fhou'd I, who never faw
 Beyond our flowery Vale ?——

He fwore that all I did was right ;
 And I, alas, believ'd :
Yet fomething wrong I acted fure,
 And therefore was deceiv'd.——

Ten Thoufand Times I call him falfe ;
 As many wifh him here :
Pay, Sifters, pay a haplefs Maid
 The tributary Tear.

An EPITAPH.

STOP, laughing Paſſenger, and turn thine Eye,
On that may change thy Mirth into a Sigh.
When thou confider'ſt he who five Feet deep,
Lies a cold Lump, in an eternal Sleep,
Was Yeſterday as gay a Thing as thou;
As little car'd for Promiſe, or for Vow.
If rich thou art, he neither wanted Pelf,
Was more content, it may be, than thyſelf.
Art young ?—art ſtrong ?—art am'rous ?—art brave ?—
Such was the Tenant of this gloomy Grave.——
Art faithful to thy Friend ?——art frank and free ?
Impatient of Controul ?——juſt ſo was he.
Yet, art thou good and mild ?—he too was ſuch.——
Art thou forgetful of the ſnarling Grutch ?
That Quality he had; and every Grace
That need adorn Succeſſors of his Race.
The Wheel of Fortune Men capricious deem :
None better underſtood the Wheel than him.
And the ſame ſteady Principles appear'd,
When in the Vale, as on the Summit rear'd.——
Art thou a Drunkard ?—to thy Shame remember,
From *January's* Month unto *December*,

He

*He ne'er was fo, tho' living among Sots;
A turnfpit Dog——and own'd by *Roger Watts.*

---

 * Poor *Sharper !* (the Memory of whom I have, from a Principle of Gratitude endeavoured to perpetuate, as having been
helped to many a good Dinner through his Means) was, at the
Time of his Death, and had been for fome Years before, the
Property of Mr. *Roger Watts,* who, at that Time, kept the Sign of
the *Cock,* in *Corn-ftreet, Briftol.*

To a young Lady, with a Pocket-Book, on Valentine's Day.

A S fair as are the Leaves of this,
  Where ne'er appear'd a Speck amiſs;
  So artleſs, and without Deſign,
  Appears to me my Valentine.

Youth, Innocence, and Gaiety,
Wit, Prudence, and Sobriety,
Their Aids together kindly join,
To decorate my Valentine.————

May every Bleſſing, every Grace
Of Mind, of Perſon, and of Face,
Increaſe ſtill more, and all combine,
To make thee lov'd, my Valentine.

Crowding Joys around thee wait,
Blaſting every evil Fate ;
And that thou ne'er have Cauſe to pine,
Is my Soul's Wiſh, my Valentine.

At

At Length, when riper Years demand,
The Comforts of the nuptial Band;
May every Virtue in him shine,
Whose happy Lot's my Valentine.————

May every Day new Pleasures yield;
Long may she sport in Plenty's Field:
And when her Breath she shall resign,
Angels receive my Valentine.

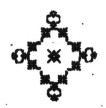

Wrote in the Gardens of *Brackenſtown*,

A Seat of Lord *Moleſworth*'s, near *Dublin*.

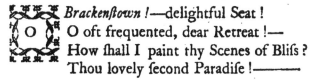 *Brackenſtown* !—delightful Seat !
O oft frequented, dear Retreat !—
How ſhall I paint thy Scenes of Bliſs ?
Thou lovely ſecond Paradiſe !————

Of *Dryden*'s Muſe had mine the Scope,
With all the nervous Strength of *Pope* ;
Like *Shakeſpear* cou'd I Nature draw ;
Whoſe Pencil ſcorn'd poetic Law,
Immortal ſhou'd thy Beauties flow,
At leaſt go Hand in Hand with * *Stowe*.——

An ancient Rookery's ſocial Noiſe
Proclaims the hoſpitable Joys,
That *Bacchus* join'd with *Ceres*, ſends,
To bleſs the beſt of Men, and Friends.————

Here may you unmoleſted rove,
Thro' flowery Lawn, or moſſy Grove :
Where Art and Nature ſtrongly vie,
And doubtful hangs the Victory.

Here thickning Honeyſuckle Bowers,
Repel the Rage of Mid-day Hours ;

---

* The Seat of Lord *Cobham*, ſo finely ſpoken of by Mr. *Pope*.

And court the Mind to contemplate
The Smiles and Frowns of fickle Fate.
Whilft fportive Birds on every Tree
Enchant with vernal Melody.

Th' induftrious Bee exerts her Strength;
Indeed fhe journeys no great Length:
For every Sweet that fhe can crave,
In her own Garden fhe may have.
Her Labours here intently view;
'Twere not amifs to copy too.————

Here waves the Elm's afpiring Head,
Beneath it creeps the Strawberry Bed.
Promifcuous fpread the Fruits and Flowers,
As in the World's firft happy Hours.————
Deck'd with a Margin Ever-Green;
A River bounds the charming Scene.————

The bleating Sheep, the lowing Steer,
The brouzing Goat,—the friendlefs Hare,
Familiar, find a Shelter here.

Adept in all, but to deceive,
Match'd with the faireft Child of *Eva*.
Here *Molefworth* dwells :————my Tafk is done,
I fain wou'd foar, but dread the Sun.————

Soon fhall we mifs thee, jolly Boy !———
That Face, the Harbinger of Joy ;
That Heart, the Fountain whence hath fprung
Such Tales as fuit not every Tongue ;
Tales worthy of an Ear that feels,
Worthy to box with Care, and kick up Sorrows Heels.

Away my antique Friend is flown,
The Silver-headed Rake is gone :
And what in *Chefter* now remains
But naufeous, melancholy Strains.———

* The Balls, that fkim along the Court,
Of Beaus, and Belles, the late Refort ;———
Seem to explain that fwift as they,
Time flies, and moulders all away,
We die To-morrow ;———fo we'll drink To-day.

The Man, who by the River *Dee*,
His own Eftate can fit, and fee ;
Whom Health, all chearing Blefling, deigns
To vifit,———he 'tis gives the Reins
To Pleafure, and the Plagues of Care difdains.

No difmal Vapours hurt the Breaft,
That is of Honefty poffeft ;
Fearlefs the Owner walks, and free ;
For dirty Bailiffs what cares he ?
O Honefty !—thou bleft, thou pleafing Sound,
So often talk'd of, and fo feldom found !

---

* The Tennis-Court, wherein the Company of Players from
London performed in the Summer Seafon of the Year 1749, under
the Direction of Mr. *Macklin*.

In Danger, if my Friend ſhould be,
And fly for Safety unto Thee ;
Tho' late, perhaps the Recreant comes,
Thou'lt ſave him from the cruel * Bums.
His wonted Quiet, to his Mind reſtore,
And ſee him ſafe on Week-days as before.————

The gloomy Dungeon I defy,
That laſt Retreat of Miſery ;—
I ſmoke my Pipe, I drink my Glaſs,
And ne'er forget my Sleep inſpiring Laſs.————

Diſpos'd to chat with pleaſant Brock,
I curſe the Time-devouring Clock ;
And now attentive, hear the Tale
Of merry *Moll*, who comes for Ale.————

If *Jones*, *Neſtorian* Sage ! ſhou'd pleaſe
To ſpeak of *Anna*'s Victories ;
Inebriated with vaſt Delight,
I hear the Cannons ;————ſee the Fight !————
And curſe the Land ingrate, that let's a Man,
Who fill'd the Trench with Blood,————now fill with Beer
    the Can.————

The Walls, the conſtant Ev'ning Walk,
I oft frequent ;—I ogle,—talk ;—
There ſteps the Nymph, whoſe cruel Eyes,
Dooms every Heart a Sacrifice :
Whoſe Smile, whoſe Frown, Speech, Silence, all alike,
With certain Death, inevitably ſtrike.

---

* A cant Term for Bailiffs.

Ladies,

Ladies, your Leave————the fqueamifh Prude,
Who conftrues every Freedom lewd,
I hate :————I hate too the Coquet,
Who fancies every Charm, and Wit,
Center in her ;————but heav'nly C——k !————
Sparkles like Meteors from the Dark.
She to the Public loft,————*Corinna* now
Reigns Goddefs of the Wall, the Street, the Row.——

Paunch-pamper'd *Bacchus* 'tis commands,
Away with Love ;————the Bottle ftands !————
The Bowl majeftic,————that improves
The palid Cheek, and warms us as it moves ————

What gen'rous Heat !—'fore gad I'm drunk !—
I'm fit for Stratagem, or Punk ;—
The Half-pint Glaffes !—thus we drink,
While puny whey-fac'd Puppies fhrink.
And fearing Spots, and ruby Nofes,
Mifcall our honeft Bumpers, Dofes.—

Of Avarice, what high Difdain,
Foments thro' ev'ry joyous Vein !————
We covet but the brighteft Lafs ;
Behold my gay o'erflowing Glafs !
I give you lovely *Lucy*——let it pafs.————

The Scene is chang'd,——and now I go
Where never enters anxious Woe.
Me * *Stanley* calls——and fay, my Mufe,
The Call of *Stanley*, who'd refufe?——
I go to what we rarely fee,
Content and Hofpitality ;
To Lady——truly good, and Brethren that agree.——

Sweetly the Hours at † *Hooton* glide,
Harmonious, gentle, free from Pride ;——
No fullen Humours harbour there,
Or fawning Tongue, or carping Care ;—
No wayward Paffions vex the Mind ;
But each is bounteous, good, and kind.——

Bright Liberty ! with fmiling Face,
Augments the Beauties of the Place ;
You fing—you drink—you walk—you chat——
And none are blam'd for this or that.——
Stanley with grateful Heart receives,
And frankly fhares what Heaven gives.——

While fome contemptuous Honours prize,
And cram their worthlefs Hearts with Lies ;
More happy his untainted Mind ;
So juftly valu'd by Mankind.—
Thro' Life I envy *Stanley*'s Part ;—
An Innocence that conquers Art.

---

* Sir *Rowland Stanley*, Knt.——Elder Branch of an ancient and
honourable Roman Catholic Family, in the Neighbourhood of
Chefter.
† The Seat of Sir *Rowland.*

A

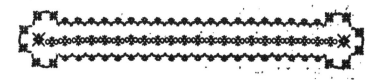

A Description of ALTIDORE,

A Seat in the County of *Wicklow*.

WHY wou'd, *O'Farrell*, you,
    Impofe a Tafk fo hard ?——
    A Tafk that might fubdue
      Apollo's favourite Bard.——
How hard, alas ! for one,
  With rough untutor'd Pen,
To paint the rifing Sun ;
  Or fing the beft of Men ?——

But, Sir, fince you command,
  Tho' fure to be undone ;
I'd take the flaming Stand,
  And fall with *Phaeton.*——
Yet, where fhall I commence ?
  I cannot bear the Sight ;
Joys crowd on ev'ry Senfe,
  And torture with Delight.——

The Swain, who *Cooper*'s Brow
  Sang fweetly heretofore ;
Had ftood amaz'd, I trow,
  At Sight of *Altidore*.

In

In *Windsor's* Praise the Muse
   Hath oft been known to soar;
A nobler Theme they chuse
   Who speak of *Altidore*.

Methinks I hear them say,
   Your rapt'rous Stuff give o'er;
And in plain Terms, I pray
   Describe us *Altidore*.
On Top of Eastern Hill,
   With Heath all cover'd o'er;
Enrich'd with many a Rill,
   Stands beauteous *Altidore*.

Your Eye commands a Plain
   Of twice Three Miles and more;
Where bask the Sheep, the Swain,
   At lovely *Altidore*.
When Novelty prevails,
   And Fields delight no more;
Survey the Clifts of *Wales*,
   From heavenly *Altidore*.

No Music there is heard,
   Save Beagles twice a Score;
And *Robin*, pretty Bird!
   That warbles *Altidore*.——
There Nature, bounteous Dame,
   Unbosoms all her Store,
And Art with conscious Shame
   Abandons *Altidore*.

No griping Cares approach ;
  No Want attends the Door ;
Or on the Joys encroach,
  Encircling *Altidore*.
And he whose godlike Heart,
  Possesses all this Store,
So tops the generous Part,
  None envy *Altidore*.——

The

The Invitation to Dr. Le Hunt's,

In the County of *Dublin*.

'TWAS early I rose, so resplendent the Day,
The Birds were deluded, and took it for *May*.
The Throstle's clear Note, eccho'd loud thro'
    the Groves,
    And the Wood-quests all round me sat cooing
    their Loves.

The Lambs newly drop'd, tho' scarce able to stand,
Yet strove to evade the fond Touch of my Hand;
By Instinct directed, so early to ken,
No Foes can approach 'em more hurtful than Men.

A Train of Reflections soon busy'd my Mind,
On Reason, the bubling Boast of Mankind;
Who tear the poor Dupe, whilst they seem to caress,
And accumulate Wealth, by each other's Distress.

With

With Mufing fatigu'd, on the Grafs I reclin'd,
Where a Brook thro' the Glen doth invitingly wind.
And as o'er the fmooth Pebbles it gently did creep,
The mufical Murmur compos'd me to fleep.

When ftrait by my Side there appear'd a fair Maid,
In Veftments as white as the Lilly array'd ;
Whofe ruddy Complexion, and Glee of whofe Face,
Shew'd Health had a fovereign Sway in the Place.

Your Cenfures are rafh, faid fhe ; Why for a few,
Should you judge the whole World to be falfe and untrue?
Come to *Branenftown Houfe, at the Top of the Hill,
And your fplenatic Humours we'll teach you to kill.

With all that the Eye can take in of Delight ;
With all that the Heart conceives virtuous and right ;
With all that brings Mirth, and gives Vapours the Rout,
I'll engage you'll be pleas'd, both within and without.

I thank'd her ; but told her, I cou'dn't that Day,
For I din'd with the 'Squire and good Mrs. Bray.
Be it foon, fhe reply'd, or I take an Affront ;
Content is my Name, and I live with *Le Hunt.

---

* Branenftown, a Seat in the County of Dublin ; the Property of
Dr. Le Hunt, formerly a Phyfician of great Eminence, but who
had retir'd from Practice fome Years before the above was wrote :
a Gentleman, who, from his extenfive Charities, Benevolence,
and great Affability, rendered himfelf juftly beloved by every
Perfon happy enough to be acquainted with him.—He is fince dead,
when the many who ftood in need of his Affiftance loft a moft valuable Benefactor ; and thofe who did not, a fincere Friend and
amiable Companion.

　　　　　　　　　　　　　　A

A S O N G.

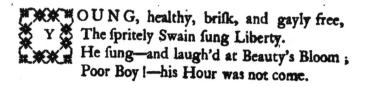OUNG, healthy, brisk, and gayly free,
The spritely Swain sung Liberty.
He sung—and laugh'd at Beauty's Bloom;
Poor Boy!—his Hour was not come.

The fair—the black—the easy Shape,
Unheeded, did his Eyes escape.
Lucinda caus'd no love-sick Gloom:
For why? his Hour was not come.

With *Sapho*, oft in Complaisance,
Of Love he'd chat—with *Chloe* dance;
Yet cold as Ice, or marble Tomb————
The fated Hour was not come.

From Opera, Route, Assembly, Play,
He bore his Heart unhurt away.
Till on a late too hapless Roam,
He *Bella* saw;————his Hour's come.————

He

He flies his Friends, his Bottle now,
Detefts his Food,—contracts his Brow;
Thofe fad Effects of *Cupid*'s Doom,
Too plain evince—the Hour's come.

Bella!——avow your Sexes Wrong;
Defpife his Sighs, his Smart prolong.
For fo fhou'd each be ferv'd, who dare
Profanely flight the lovely Fair.——

An EPILOGUE,

In the Character of a Lieutenant of a Privateer
regailing his Crew.

Spoke by Mrs. *Green*, at her Benefit at *Jacob's
Well* Theatre, *Bristol*, 1759.

 OME, bear a Hand——and put the Ladle
   round,——
C Yo-ho! the t'other Bowl!———we're all
   aground.
   Health to great *George*, and *Prussia's* valiant
   King:
   A Cheer my Lads, and make the Ceiling
   ring.
        Huzza! Huzza!

Well play'd, my Hearts of Oak, my *Bristol* Boys!——
To scare a *Frenchman*!——that's your only Noise.
Long have we reign'd the Sov'reigns of the Main;
Oft have we thump'd the Fleets of *France* and *Spain*;
And when they dare come out,——we'll do't again.

O

O for an *Indiaman* now, Homeward bound !——
And d——n the Dog that flinches t'other Round.
'Till *British* Colours stream from *Gallic* Staff.
And we, as Winners, have a Right to Laugh.——

Laden with Plunder, then we'd boldly come,
To our own * *Marshstreet,* and carouse at Home.
Full Bowls——full Dishes——Jollity and Fun ;
Safe from the Chain Shot, or the Swivel Gun.

Such is the Life we jovial Sailors lead :
Freely we drink and love ;——as freely bleed.
When Merchants need us, that are just and kind,
And brave Commanders,——who wou'd lag behind?——

Each fills his Keg, and to the † *Gib* he scowers ;
Gives *Moll* a Smack, and tips her Will and Powers.
She, blubbering, begs a little longer Stay ;
Off goes the Boat,——and we are under Way.——

Come fill us round,——and leave no Room for Lip,——
Luck to the *Bristol* ;————she's a gallant Ship !——
To ‡ *Dipden* Fortune wheresoe'er he steers ;
And may *France* dread the *English* Privateers.
Huzza ! Huzza !

---

* A Street, with regard to *Bristol,* as *Wapping* and *Rotherhith* are
to *London,*————for the Reception of Sailors; &c. and supplying
them with Slops.——

† The *Gib,*————a Ferry at the End of *Prince's-street,* where
Sailors, &c. take Boat, to go on Board their Ships in *Kingroad.*

‡ The Commander, at that Time, of the *Bristol* Privateer.

A

A BALLAD.

IT is not for *Polly*, it is not for *Ann*,
It is not for *Marg'et*, it is not for *Fann*;
It is not for *Lucy*,————for *Sally* I vex,
But the *Je ne fcai quoi* that belongs to the Sex.

The Pride of *Amanda* I view with an Eye,
That laughs at the Puppies, who whimper and figh.
For Reafon thus dictates,————be frolic, my Boy;
Grief is not the Paffport to *Je ne fcai quoi !*

The Witty, the Pretty, the Wanton, the Prude,
The dignify'd Lady, the Villager rude,
My paffionate Raptures coequal employ,
For all are Difpenfers of *Je ne fcai quoi!*

Ye Dabblers in Metre, Retailers of Dreams,
With your Garlands of Willow, and murmuring Streams;
A Plague o' your Nonfenfe, fuch Dampers of Joy
Ought never to tafte of the *Je ne fcai quoi.*

Are

Are ye fearful to fail, when the Fair ye purfue?
Call o' *Tomkins*, and throw down a Bumper or Two.
Dull Meagrims, there's nought like *Champagne* to
      deftroy;
'Tis the fhorteft of Cuts to the———*Je ne fcai quoi.*

On

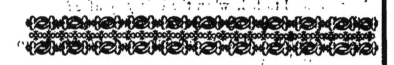

On seeing a Group of Ladies

Very curious in their Infpection of the Mechanifm
of Mr. *Ladd*, of *Trowbridge*, his Machine, con-
ftructed to travel without Horfes, by the Means
of what he term'd an *Endlefs Chain*; exhibited
at *Cock*'s Auction Room, *Spring Garden*, 1759
and allowed by the Nobility, Gentry and Mechanics, who came in great Numbers to fee it, to
be the moft compleat Piece of Mechanifm they
had ever met with : The Chain (for which Mr.
Ladd, the Inventor, hath obtained his Majefty's
Patent for Fourteen Years) being applicable to
Cranes, Sugar-Mills, and many other Purpofes,
in order to fave Labour, both with Regard to
Men and Cattle, &c.

W HEN no Recefs I find's fecure,
    Not even the fcientific *Scene*,
'Gainft Beauty's bright tranfporting Lure;
    The Ladies crowd to *Ladd*'s Machine.

Sage *Ladd*, refolve whate'er they afk ;
For know each Eye contains an Elf,
Shall find it but a trifling Tafk
To turn thy Force againft thyfelf.——

With Smiles they now can pufh us on,
   And back us with their Frowns again;
But one Point more, and we're undone :
   They only want the endlefs Chain.————

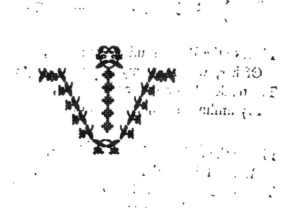

A

A BALLAD.

Sung by Mr. *Vernon.*

'T WAS underneath a *May*-blown Bush,
    Where Violets sprang, and sweet Primroses;
With Voice melodious as the Thrush,
    So *Johnny* sung, collecting Poesies.

These to the Breast must be convey'd,
  Of her, who sways my warmest Fancy;
The tender, blooming, artless Maid,
  My smiling, mild, good-natur'd *Nancy.*——

I know the Suburb Youths will jeer,
  And call me witless Oaf and Zany;
That I from constant Heart declare,
  I ne'er will love, except my *Nanny.*

I envy them nor Pomp nor Dress,
  Or Conquests gain'd, o'er Hearts of many:
The Study of my Life's to bless,
  And please my dear, my grateful *Nanny.*——

Oh

Oh! how unlike, my Fair, to thofe
  Whofe wanton Charms are free to any ;———
I'd give the World could I difclofe ,
  One fiftieth Part the Worth of *Nanny*.———

Let Bucks, and Bloods, in burnt Champagne,
  Toaft *Lucy, Charlotte, Poll* or *Fanny* ;
At Notions, fo abfurdly vain,
  I fmile, and clafp my blamelefs *Nanny*.

A BALLAD.

LET *Hayman, Hudson, Worlidge* paint
  The Dames of Town or Valley;
Their warmeſt Beauties are but faint,
  Compar'd to thoſe of *Sally.*

Ye Bucks and Beaux, with jemmy Cloaths,
  Who rant, and rake, and rally;———
With *Nell* and *Poll,* and Drabs like thoſe,
  You'll never do for *Sally.*

Her Eyes are black, and pierce ſo quick,
  'Tis dang'rous Work to dally;———
I'm ſure I ne'er was half ſo ſick
  As I've been made by *Sally.*

Her Shape is ſtrait, her Boſom white:
  Deſcribe her full, how ſhall I?
All that can give ſupreme Delight,
  Exiſts at once in *Sally.*

But

But, curse on Fortune's fickle Plan,
   Whilst Kings might Fight for *Sally* ;
Why will she keep the *Naked Man*,
   And live in *Black Boy Alley* ?——

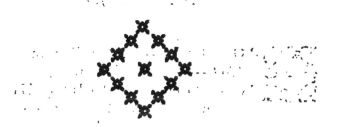

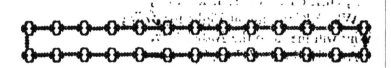

On being prefent at a great Meeting of
PSALM-SINGERS,

To perform at O——e, near B——l, on *Sunday*,
the 29th of *June*.

FROM focial D——'s friendly Farm,
 To O——e's Church we rode;
Where, to protect our Souls from Harm,
 We heard the Word of God.——

Chaunters, from far and near, that Day
 Had been for Months expected;
And *Johns* and *Joans*, as blith as *May*,
 In Crowds were there collected.

On Horfes lame and blind they came,
 And fome on Foot did run;
And there was Ale, and Cakes, and Game:
 'Twas to a Wake almoft.

S——'s rev'rend Subftitute was dull;
  The C——k had bung'd his Eyes;
The Weather hot, the Church brimfull:
  I thought 'twas Time to rife.

No, whifper'd *Ben*, althof I'm toir'd
  Of Stuff not worth a Farthing;
I may'nt go out; 'twull be admoir'd,
  Becafe I'm now Churchwareden.

But look amangft our Pews, and zay,
  If in ale *Briftol* Zitty,
Girls may be vound zo brifk, and gay,
  Zo taper, and zo pretty ?——

Around I threw my wand'ring Eyes,
  And tho' in Courts they've been,
I there declare without Difguife,
  More charming was the Scene.

A native Innocence there reign'd
  In ev'ry blooming Face :
Superior Praifes none obtain'd,
  For each had equal Grace.

Sure never were fo fair a Set,
  Affembl'd in a Ring;
Nor e'er before fuch Angels met,
  To hear fuch Mortals fing.

To

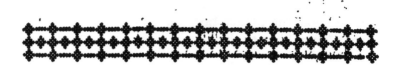

To my BED.

Tranſlated from the *French.*

THeatre of Smiles and Tears,
Where firſt began, where end our Cares;
Well thou ſhew'ſt us how near Neighbours
Are our Pleaſures and our Labours.

Advice

Advice to Mr. Benjamin Sedgly,

At the Time thefe Lines were firft wrote, Mafter of the *Ship and Anchor* Alehoufe at *Temple-Bar*, who fubfcribed himfelf Author of a Poem on feeing a Collection of Pictures done by Mr. *Worlidge*; and likewife of a Pamphlet againft that of Mr. *Fielding's*, relative to Street-Robbers.

By Mr. Solomon Lanham,

At the fame Time Mafter of the *Blue Pofts* Alehoufe, *Covent-Garden.*

WHO wou'd his Patron's Intellects degrade,
And blaft his Folly, while he eats his Bread?—
Or with the learned Counfel of his Plea,
Conteft the Juftice of the well-known Fee?
Who, rifing from right reverend Table, full,
Wou'd tell his Lordfhip his Difcourfe was dull?
Or, with the Ladies hopes to make his Way,
By cenfuring all they act, and all they fay?
In Shape imperfect,—or if Reafon halt;
Sage *Ben*, be hufh!—none love to hear the Fault.——
So tender is the Age;——and 'tis but Sport,
Who thinks, by Truth, to raife himfelf at Court.——

Even

Even Panygeric fhou'd with Art be fram'd,
And not with fulfome Hyperbolics cramm'd.——
Great Souls by Flatt'ry cannot be mifled,
They loath the Dunghil where the Maggot bred.
Hark to thy Good!—miftaken Man, ——attend
The warm Remonftrance of a Brother—Friend,——
Who hopes no Inter'ft from his Care may flow,
More than thy Safety from impending Woe.——
Ne Sutor ultra Crepidam, you know,
Directs each Man how far he ought to go ;
And when they ftep beyond fuch ftated Brink,
Like you they flounder, 'till like you they fink.——
O had you but your Name-fake's Share of Glee,
Well might'ft thou then contend in Poetry :
Or had the *Irifh* Deans vaft Store of Wit
Supply'd thee from its Sweepings, fimple Cit,
Much from thy Works, and juftly might we hope ;
And Fifty *Sedgley*'s might compofe a *Pope*.
But as Things are, nor Satyrs Depth explore,
Nor aim at Wit ;——but take your Chalk and fcore ;——
Let *Worlidge* paint, and *Fielding* write in Peace ;
Blunder you on, in Ignorance, and Greafe.——
The greateft Bards their ill Succefs have had ;
What can'ft thou hope, fo execrably bad ?——
Froward the Mufes, ——to thy Suit unkind,
Pufh up to Fortune, fhe, good Lady's blind ;
And, haply may give Ear ;——quit humourous Strokes,
And cut Rump-fteak's, inftead of cutting Jokes.——
To force the Smile, or draw the tender Tear,
Is not for thee, *Ben*,——ftick to drawing Beer,
And fix thy Anchor of Dependance there.
When thou haft Time for't, hear what others fay ;
Some Salt here, Boy !——You've Twenty-pence to pay.
You're welcome, Sir !——Walk, Gentlemen, this Way.

Three

Three Mutton-pies, you Rafcal ;—how you ftare !—
Welfh Rabbit ?---Yes, Sir ;---*Molly*---mind the Bar ;
Befs Adams, Sir, was hang'd with Lawyer *Carr*.———
This is enough for you and I, d'ye fee ;
A Pox, O ! Science———and Philofophy.———
I recommend the Modes myfelf have try'd,
And fee Wits walk, whilft I triumphant ride.

On seeing the PATENT MACHINE,

Now exhibited at *Cock's* Auction Room, *Spring Gardens*, invented by Mr. *John Ladd*, of *Trowbridge*.

FAR, far away, Rancour!---Stupidity dream on;
Foul Envy avaunt! thou implacable Dœmon!---
Your Powers connected, he need not to fear,
Whose Carriage is blamelefs, from Principles clear.
So well think Mankind of the Patent Machine;
The Odds, among Sporters, run high againft * *Green.*
Full well they're convinc'd of its winning the Day,
Since Merit gives Motion, and Fame clears the Way.

---

* Mr. *Green* of *Maidenhead*; with whom Mr. *Ladd* had made a Bett of 200 *l.* that his Machine fhould run One Hundred Miles in lefs Time than Mr. *Green* fhould perform it with a Poft-Chaife and a Pair of the ableft Horfes he could put to it.

A BALLAD,

Wrote immediately after the Engagement at *St. Cas*,

YE Soldiers and Sailors, to both I indite,
As Children of *Britain*, be Brethren in Fight ;
Let Jealousies die, and no more disagree,
Ye Lords of the Land, and ye Lords of the Sea.
For such are the Titles each Annal bestows,
On the Bulwarks of *Britain*, and Scourge of her Foes.

Remember the Gallantry shewn at *St. Cas*,
A parallel Action the Sun never saw ;
Where about Fifteen Hundred of stout Grenadiers,
Fill'd the whole *Gallic* Army with ague-like Fears :
As impregnable Forts, by each other they stood,
'Till disfigur'd with Wounds, and half drowned in Blood.

With Grief let me add, O perpetual Shame
To a barb'rous Nation, the Outcast of Fame !—
O'erpower'd and broke, when for Quarter they su'd,
French Swords to the Hilts in their Hearts were embru'd.
Remember this, Soldiers, the next Time you meet,
And second them well, ye brave Boys of the Fleet.

Our

Our young gallant * Prince was on Shore all the while,
Experienc'd an Enemy savage and vile ;——
He saw his best Troops, (Want of Powder and Ball)
All scatter'd like Sheep——saw their General fall †;
Your Favourite, ye Guards !---O may Peace ne'er be made,
'Till his Blood, and your own, at *St. Cas* be repaid.

---

* His royal Highness *Edward* Duke of *York.*
† General *Dury*, who fell by a Musket Shot, in his Retreat to
the Boats.

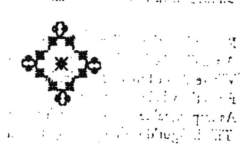

An EPILOGUE,

After appearing in the Character of the MOCK
DOCTOR, at *Jacob's Well* Theatre, *Briſtol*.

THIS Night you have ſeen me, ſore againſt my
Will,
Severely drubb'd into a Man of Skill;
From Faggot-binder, Lud !—how quick I've ſped,
Reſtor'd the Sick, the Lame, the Blind, the Dead ;
Or, if I have not, it has ſo been ſaid :
And that's ſufficient———many a daring Man,
Now boaſts a Fortune from the ſelf-ſame Plan ;
Puffs well prepar'd are of amazing Uſe ;
Where One rejects, ten ſwallow the Abuſe.
Hence the Increaſe of rev'rend *W———d*'s Stores ;
And hence licentiate *R—ck* in gilded Chariot ſnores.
A Doctor now, without the Aid of Rules,
The Pedantry of Colleges or Schools,
Have at another Trade, without the Tools.
I'll Poetry commence, turn Mind's Director,
And rival Brother *John*, the learn'd Inſpector :
Keen cutting Satyr write ; but firſt I'll hie
Far, far from *Briſtol* ;——hear the Reaſon why !——
Whilſt Induſtry appears in every Face ;
Whilſt Truth your Men, Virtue your Women grace ;

Whilſt

Whilſt Friendſhip, Honour, Loyalty and Love,
Are the main Springs by which your Actions move;
Whilſt Avarice, Sloth, Hypocriſy and Lies,
With every Crime, obnoxious to the Wiſe,
Ye are known to abhor, what Room for Satyr here?
Truth muſt expunge, tho' Rancour ſhou'd beſmear.
Yet e're I go,—permit me take my Leave;
With theſe, my Thanks, for Favours paſt, receive;
Acknowledgment, the Player's all,——I give——
May Heaven increaſe your Wealth, your Peace, your
      Stores;
The greateſt Good to me, will be to hear of yours.

A BALLAD.

SWEETER than the sweetest Muse,
Breaths the Maid whom *Damon* sues.
Than Snow her whiter Bosom heaves;
Damon swears,——the Maid believes.

Straiter than the Mountain Pine
Is her Shape; her Air divine;
Eyes more piercing than the Sun;
Damon swears!——the Maid's undone.——

Innocent, and youthful Fair,
Objects of my tenderest Care:
O beware the flattering Smile;
Of trickling Tear, the study'd Guile.

Him suspect that wou'd persuade,
Ye are more than mortal made;
Weigh your Men by Virtue's Rules,
Think who break them, worst of Fools.

On a MILLER,

In Love with Two pretty young Ladies.

G O Tool of State,
  And ſcratch thy Pate,
And tear thy Lungs to Tatters:
  Now in, now out,
  Take t'other Bout;
I ſing of Country Matters.

  The Court, 'tis true,
  Has Charms for you;
But take it not in Joke, Sir;
  When I declare,
  Your String and Star
Mere Baubles are at S———ke, Sir.

  Ambition here,
  Did ne'er appear;
Your Sun-ſhine we deſpiſe, Sir;
  We have all we aſk,
  When we can baſk
In *Poll* and *Betſey's* Eyes, Sir.

Thofe lovely Maids,
To Mafquerades,
Altho' they've not been bred, Sir ;
In rural Dance,
Might challenge *France*,
And put their Dames to Bed, Sir.

Like Light'ning fhine
Their Eyes divine,
They're ftrait and handfome grown, Sir ;
And tho' you fee,
No Lady *B*———,
Their Faces are their own, Sir.

At *M*———'s Stream,
They're ftill my Theme ;
And in the 'Squire's Park, Sir,
To give me Eafe,
I fpoil the Trees,
By carving it on Bark, Sir.———

O *V—n—t* why
Are not you I ?
For then I cou'd go boldly ;———
But old and poor,
They'd fhut the Door,
And ufe the Miller coldly.———

H   When

When * Flagellet,
Tell *Poll* and *Bet*,
The Prieft has done his Duty;
Their Court'fies made,
Each killing Jade
Removes her Fund of Beauty:

I ftay behind,
I gaze on Wind;———
Till blind as Ma—d—'s Thiller;———
Then, bang the Gate,
And curfe the Fate,
Of feeble *Mull* the Miller.

---

* The Inftrument made ufe of to play the Congregation out of
Church, inftead of an Organ.

A BALLAD.

I.

SISTER Nymphs, by a Maiden forlorn,
    Difdain not Example to take ;——
Since a Swain fure yet never was born,
    So true as I late did forfake.——

II.

How oft has he, all the Day long,
    To Love in foft Accents me prefs'd ;——
While the Lark, ftopping fhort at his Song,
    My Youth's fofter Notes hath confefs'd.——

III.

Ah, how bleft had I been at this Time,
    Had I not fell a Victim to Pride ?——
Then take heed whilft you bloom in your Prime,
    And remember the Caufe that I dy'd.——

IV.

IV.

To become a gay Toast of the Town,
  My poor Shepherd and Lambs I forsook;
My Cot, and my grey russet Gown;
  My Innocence, Dog, and my Crook,

V.

To another now *Damon* is flown,
  Whose Faith is superior to mine;
Fate bless them——whilst round my sad Stone,
  The Willow and Cypress entwine.

AN-

ANOTHER.

I.

RECLIN'D on a Hillock of wild Thyme fo fweet,
My Kids nibling round me, my Dog at my Feet;
The Sky-lark and Throſtle beguil'd me of Pains,
And my Pipe I laid by to attend to their Strains.

II.

But what Joys are complete, when my *Peggy's* away?
How I ſigh'd, and I languiſh'd for thee, as I lay !——
My Temples the Sun-beams moſt forely did heat;
The God perhaps anger'd I wiſh'd his Retreat.

III.

Fatigu'd thus in Mid-day, to *Somnus* I pray'd,
As foon as invok'd, he flew fwift to my Aid ;——
A Blifs next to Heaven difclos'd to my View,
For with him he brought the Refemblance of you.

H 3   IV.

IV.

But long I enjoy'd not the fweeteft of Scenes,
Too rudely difturb'd by the cruel'ft of Means;
A Wolf lank with Famine from Foreft there came,
And bore off thy Gift—my poor favourite Lamb.

V.

As quick as the Light'ning, I chas'd the foul Thief,
By Paffion inflam'd, and prick'd forward by Grief;
The dear little Bleater I refcu'd from Death,
And left its grim Foe without Motion or Breath.

VI.

Impute not my Abfence to any falfe Tale,
Might efcape to the Brow, from the Buz of the Vale;
Believe it rank Envy at Sight of fuch Twain,
The faireft of Fair, and the faithfulleft Swain.

On *seeing* Mr. Ladd's *Machine to go without* Horfes.

SAYS Fortune to Time, prithee what art about?
This *Trowbridge* Machine makes a terrible Rout.
We muftn't thus fuffer, my politic Brother,
One Tradefman fo much to annoy all the other.
With thy Scythe prithee ftop his intended Career,
Or he'll fteal all the Arts, one by one, we may fear.
But Virtue that dotes on a Heart without Crime,
Shall fupport thee, O *Ladd*, againft Fortune and Time.

On

On the *sudden Death of Mr.* DRAPER,

Late Bookseller in the *Strand.*

ESTEEM'D by Strangers, and by Friends belov'd;
By Merit's Touchstone, G——k's self approv'd;
Sought by the Wretched, as a sure Relief;
And by the Happy, as a Foe to Grief;——
On whose frank Brow still grew the honest Smile,
Fruit of a Heart incapable of Guile;————
Sage were his Sentiments,—his Dictates mild;
Of Spirit harmless, as the new-born Child;
So *Draper* liv'd, and as he liv'd he dy'd,
Not roughly torn, but gently drawn aside.
Heaven wou'd his spotless Sail shou'd rest close furl'd, ⎫
E're Billows boil, Rocks rend, and Flames be hurl'd; ⎬
To scourge the black Remains of an ungrateful World ⎭

A BALLAD.

Sung at *Sadler's Wells*, ———— the Mufic by Mr.
Patterfal.

I.

THO yonder Beech's friendly Shade
Repair, fair *Aura*, lovely Maid,
And whilft our Lambkins frolick make,
My rural Prefents dein to take.

II.

Were to my Wifh thy Temples bound,
How Eaftern Gems fhould blaze around ?———
Yet Wifhes are but idle Breath,
In lieu, behold a Primrofe Wreath !———

III.

Were both the *Indies* at my Beck,
I'd ranfack both my Nymph to deck.
But as it is, vouchfafe to wear
What once enwrapt my fleecy Care.

IV.

IV.

Of burnifh'd Gold, or Silver fair,
Thofe Feet of thine fhou'd Sandals bear ;
But all I have I offer now,
The Hide of *Dap*, my favourite Cow !

V.

Said *Aura*, Sandals, Robes, and Crowns,
Are flender Proofs 'gainft Fortune's Frowns ;
We've Health and Eafe ;——is Heaven fcant ?——
Here—take my Hand——we've all we want.

On *seeing a Bust of the Marquis of* Granby, *at Mr.* Rackstrow's, *Statuary, in* Fleet-street.

WHEN such Resemblance of their Chief they see,
Loud roar the uncap'd Crowd, and bend the
Knee;
     Revere the good,—the loyal,—brave and just,
The generous honest Marquis !—'tis his Bust:
But well may they mistake a nice Design,
That wants but Breath, O Jove, to stamp it thine.

Pastoral DUET.

H E.

LOUD proclaims the Blackbird's Note,
Rigid Winter's chang'd his Coat;
The Throstle, Linnet, Finch and Dove,
On budding Sprays renew their Love.
Sweet *Philomel* begins to sing,
And every Fly on gilded Wing,
Hails the bright Sun, and each upbraid
Thee, too reserv'd hard-hearted Maid !——

S H E.

The Birds from whom your Proofs you take,
Love, I grant,——but ne'er forsake ;
Poor *Philomela*'s plaintiff Cry,
Bears Record of Man's Perfidy ;
Your painted Flies of various Hue,
Are wavering spotted Types of you ;
And Eccho, loudly as she can,
Sobs horrid Tales of cruel Man.——

H E.

H E.

With worſe than Steel, ah, do not ſtrike
A Heart, to others moſt unlike ;
By Rules of Art, I ne'er cou'd ſay ;
No Nymph but you, e'er heard me pray ;—
Believe by this extorted Tear—
Ah me !—You know my Soul ſincere.—

S H E.

Inconſtant as Ship-mocking Gale,
Fantaſtic as a Fairy Tale ;
I have ſtill eſteem'd the idle Breath,
That whin'd out Daggers, Darts, and Death ;
Me, Coxcombs ever did offend ;
One cannot make a Fool, a Friend ;
'Tis prudence takes thy honeſt Part,
I to thy Virtues yield my Heart.

A BALLAD.

I LAY, and dream'd on *Polly*'s Face,
For which e'en *Jove* might quit his Place ;
Her charming Shape, her cruel Eye,
Difdainful of the Lover's Sigh ;
When whifper'd Time,——Thou Fool take Heart,
My Sand repels the Urchin's Dart.——

I'll fweep the Bloom from off the Fruit,
  The Rofes fcatter dead and pale ;
Too late then each revolted Suit,
  She fhall bemoan, when Beauties fail.——
The Magic broke, fhe foon fhall be
Defpis'd by All,——but moft by thee.——

I 'woke, I found my Heart at reft ;
I now difcharge thee from my Breaft ;
Proceed awhile to vex Mankind,
But, perjur'd fair One, hope to find
    No more Dominion o'er my Mind,
        I take my laft Adieu !

I now can fmile at all your Arts,
Defy the keeneft of Love's Smarts,
And hence will try Ten Thoufand Hearts
        E're dote again on you.

A

A BALLAD,

Sung by *Andrews*, in the Character of a *Somerset-*
shire Farmer's Son,

I.

COME *Realph*, come *Robin* and *Zue*,
  And lift to the Words I do zoy;
  A Stary I'll tell you as true
  As the Bible wherein ye do proy.
We veather to *Lunnun* ye kna
 I been to zell Bearly and Kine;
And I dan't keare how aft I do go,
 The Pleace be zo woundily vine.

II.

The Mearketing aver and done,
 A Butcher as vine as a Lord,
Zware damun he'd zhaw us zome Vun,
 And 'ifaith ware as good as his Word.
He took us whare Lions do lie,
 At a Heaufe that Valks kaled the Tower,
 Wee rauring they terrify'd I,
I ware glad to get out again, zhower.

III.

III.

From therehence to Pallace we went,
  And his Majefty, God blefs his Greace,
Ware gawing to his Parliament,
  Zo I gut'n a Zoight of his Feace.
Awoy then to *Weftminfter Abbey*,
  Where ale the dead Quality loies;
And a Vellow, tho' clathed but zhabby,
  Zung Hiftories wondrous woife.

IV.

To Dinner we afterwards went;
  Beft Drink ware as plenty as Whoy:
And to ftitch up the whole Merriment,
  They zhaw'd me a Pleace kal'd a Ploy.
And there ware a Mon in Difguife,
  A little * old zorrowful King,
That made the Valk cry out their Eyes,
Thof they knew he ware no fick a thing.

V.

The next Day my jolly good Vrends,
  Had us up unto *Zadler's Wells*;
Whare no Mon need gride what ah fpends,
  Cafe it ale other Peaftime excells.
Lads and Laffes do deance on a Coord,
  And tumble, and plaay ye fick Tricks,
Methough aftentime by the Loord,
  The Taads wou'd ha braken their Necks.

---

* King *Lear*.

VI.

VI.

Wawnds and Blid! they do keaper zo hoigh,
  O Laud!——'tis ameazing to think ;——
And if you do chance to be droy,
  You may ha whatfomdever you'll drink.
If e'er ye to *Lunnun* do gaw,
  Zee *Zadler's Wells*, I do proy ;
You'll loike it, I very wele knaw ;
  'Tis better by Half nor the Ploy.

A SONG.

O N the Bank of the *Isis* she sat,
    Maria, the much injur'd Fair;
    Who too soon by the Caprice of Fate,
    Had fallen to *Lycidas'* Share.

To the Clouds the sad Plaintive addres'd,
    The Mountains re-eccho'd her Moan;
And *Juno*, the Queen of the Blest,
    Deep felt for those Pangs oft Her own.——

To the Nymph strait her Sister she sent,
    Minerva, the Chaste, and the Wise;
And with her she carry'd *Content*,
    The only true Balm of the Skies.

What Time that the love-sick poor Maid,
    Thought Poison she'd reach'd to her Lip,
In lieu of't the Goddess convey'd
    Her Tincture, which *Polly* did sip.——

To her Eyes then did Slumber return;
    The faithless ones brought to her View;
She saw the vile Perjurers burn,
    And saw them with Carelessness too.

Blest

Bleft with Peace in her Bofom fhe wak'd,
   From Dream like a Babe newly born ;————
Thinks no more of her Tendernefs wreck'd,
   Except 'tis with Horror and Scorn.————

For fhe fees now Mankind as they are ;
   Maria fees *Lycidas*' Plain ;
And regrets but her Prudence and Care,
   Long loft on fo worthlefs a Swain.————

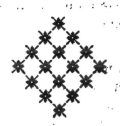

A SONG.

 N OT. by bleak Winds or nipping Froft,
    Or ruder Hand of clownifh Swain,
    My fav'rite Rofe, I lately loft;
    No fairer Flower grac'd the Plain.————

In vain the Dews of fragrant Morn,
    Befprinkl'd o'er its drooping Head;
E're Noon it fell,—was fcatter'd,—torn,———
    By Reptile murder'd, it had bred.————

So doth it fare with maiden Breaft,
    Where Love hath once poffefs'd a Part;
A cruel Tafk to guard the reft,
    The Traitor Pity yields the Heart.

She, who ne'er knew what Paffion meant,
    But Lambkins tends in rural State;
Muft keep out Love, or fweet Content;
    Abandons, aye, her Father's Gate.

The CHIMNEY-SWEEPER.

Sung by Mr. *Atkins* at *Sadler's Wells.*

 N various Shapes I have oft been known,
  To pleafe your Ears and Eyes ;
  Nor I the only one in Town,
  That wears the black Difguife.
     Sweep! Sweep!——
    Sweep, Soot ho !

In fpite of Mocks, or Flouts, or Fleers,
 A Truth I muft impart ;
No Chimney half fo foul appears,
 As doth the human Heart.
     Sweep! Sweep ! &c.

The learned Lawyers cou'd I win
 To give their Briefs to me ;
From foul Demurs, and many a Sin,
 My Brufh fhou'd fet them free.
    Sweep ! Sweep ! &c.

      Obferve

Obferve the Doctors as they roll,
    To fcrape from all Degrees ;
Much Sweeping wants each footy Soul,
    All clogg'd with filthy Fees.
                     Sweep! Sweep! &c.

Beyold yon Prieft, fo neat and trim,
    That vicious reverend Beau !———
There's no fuch Thing as cleanfing him,
    The Devil and I do know.
                     Sweep! Sweep! &c.

The Statefman with that Brow fevere,
    Had been as well forgot ;———
His Confcience is as Ermin clear,
    And therefore needs me not.
                     Sweep! Sweep! &c.

The

The JOLLY TAR.

Sung at *Sadler's Wells*.

W HY not to the * Bridge Foot venture?——
Rot the Gang!—odfblood, I'll enter ;
Not like lazy Lubbard roam,
To cheat the King, and fkulk at Home.——
Lal, lal, &c.

To gallant *Gilcbrift*, now on Shore,
I'll take myfelf, and twenty more.
He, *Watfon*, and *Bofcawen* too,
They know full well what we can do.——
Lal, lal, &c.

What, *Harry! Jack!*——I'm glad you're come ;
Moll, bear a Hand, and fetch the Rum ;———
Thou'rt almoft gone, my honeft Kag ;
Here's to *Britannia*'s flying Flag.
Lal, lal, &c.

---

* The Sign of the *Bear*, at the Foot of *Weftminfter* Bridge, a
Houfe of Rendezvous.

And to each Captain bold and true,
Who ftands by us, as I by you.
We'll lump them all who bear Command ;
But, pox o'Cowards, Sea and Land.

Lal, lal, &c.

Here's to the never-flinching Tar,
And to a fmart and glorious War ;
And to each kind good-natur'd Wench :
O blefs the King !————and d———n the *French.*

Lal, lal, &c.

The RESOLVE.

A BALLAD.

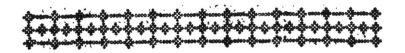

F**OR** ever accurſt may I wander forlorn,
Nor dare to look up to the Face of the Morn;
If e'er I repeal the determin'd Adieu——
What a Wretch muſt he be who can dote upon
  you ?——

Whoe'er hath obſerv'd a poor Linnet diſtreſs'd,
Her young ones ſcarce fledg'd, newly ſtole from the Neſt ?
Such Pangs felt my Heart at our final Adieu;
What a Wretch was I then ſo to dote upon you ?—

But Wiſdom appear'd, and bade Folly be gone,
Brought Smiles to my Brow, and far chas'd away Moan;
A lovely one gave me, ſweet temper'd and true,
And we laugh at the Dupe that can dote upon you.——

By Fancy miſled, ah ! how ſimple are thoſe,
Who ſmell to the Crocus, and ſpurn at the Roſe ?
Such a Thing was myſelf, till you forc'd the Adieu;
And ſuch muſt be each who can dote upon you.

A

A Hunting S O N G.

Introduced in the last new Pantomime at *Sadler's Wells*, called *Harlequin Deserter.*

Sung by Mr. *Andrews.*

RECITATIVE.

THE whistling Ploughman hails the blushing Dawn,
The Thrush melodious joins th' uncooth Salute;
Loud sings the Blackbird thro' resounding
    Groves;
High soars the Lark to meet the rising Sun.—

AIR.

Away to the Copse, lead away,
  And now, my Boys, throw off the Hounds;
I warrant he shews us some Play;
  See yonder he skulks o'er the Grounds!———
Give your Coursers the Spur then, and smoke 'em, my
    Bloods,
  'Tis a delicate Scent-lying Morn;
What Concert is equal to this of the Woods,
  'Twixt Eccho, the Hound, the Horn.
           What Concert, &c.
           'Twixt Eccho, &c.

Each

Each Earth, fee, he tries at in vain;
   The Covert no fafer can find;
So he breaks it, and fcowers amain.
   And leaves us a Diftance behind.——
O'er Rocks, Hills and Hedges, and Rivers, we fly,
   All Hazards and Dangers we fcorn;
Stout *Reynard* we'll follow until that he die:————
   Chear up the good Dogs with the Horn.——

And now he fcarce creeps thro' the Dale;
   See his Brufh, how it drops!——fee his Tongue!——
His Speed can no longer avail;
   Who of late was fo cunning and ftrong.————
From our ftaunch and fleet Pack, 'twas in vain that he fled,
   See they tear him,—bemir'd—forlorn——
The Farmers, with Pleafure, behold him lie dead,
   And fhout to the Sound of the Horn.

The Country Wife.

A S O N G.

I.

 IRTUE doſt thou praiſe, and Truth?
Simple, inconſiſtent Youth!
Prudence tells me, little loth
Wou'dſt thou be to ruin both.————

II.

Waſte not then thy Time on me;
Too, too plain the Hook I ſee;
But know, a Wiſh yet never ſtray'd,
Beyond my Shepherd, Flock, and Shade.

III.

What the Boaſt of Wealth, and Race,
Of Pride, of Luxury, and Place;
When Conſcience inward turns the Eye,
Nor lets one Act uncenſur'd by?————

IV.

IV,

Follow thou Ambition's Lot,
I've all I prize within my Cot;
Go tell the tinfell'd Dames at Court,
I make of them, and thee, my Sport,

V.

Vaunt from plighted Vow fincere;
How oft you ftrove my Soul to tear?
But do me Juftice then, and tell,
How much unlike a modern Belle!

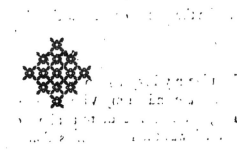

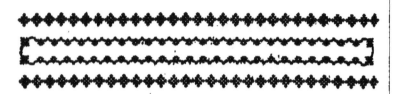

A CANTATA.

RECITATIVE.

T H E Sun had flipt behind the Weftern Hill ;
The ruddy Swain had penn'd the bleating Lambs;
The Lark had funk to reft, the Doves were
perch'd,
When the Grove eccho'd with fad plaintive Notes.

AIR.

Indulge my Prayer immortal *Jove!*
  For me and all my Virgin Throng ;
Bright Wifdom fend, to banifh Love :
  Such was the foft *Licetta*'s Song.

RECIT.

Left Heaven fhou'd grant a Suit fo well prefer'd,
The *Paphian* Boy, adept in fubtle Wiles,
Sent young *Lyfander*, Swain of pleafing Form,
Who thus, with foothing Air, the Maid addrefs'd.

AIR.

Milder than the *April* Morn,
   Than Lillies fairer, fweet thou art;
Teach not to thy Brow a Scorn,
   That Nature never meant thy Heart.
Let me lead thee from a Place,
   Fit only for the Soul difeas'd;
Joys on Joys await that Face ——
   She fmil'd Affent —— and Love was pleas'd.

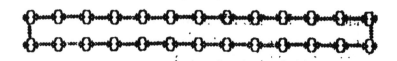

A SONG,

Sung by Mr. *Atkins* at *Sadler's Wells*, in the Character of *Charon*.

I.

A Plague on the *English* Commanders, for me,
North and South, Eaft and Weſt, from the Land
and the Sea,
They mow down ſuch Heaps of the raſcally *French*,
I'm as ſick of my Boat, as a Judge of his Bench.

II.

I wiſh on their Swords I cou'd fix but a Spell ;
There isn't a Grain of true Comfort in Hell.
In ſuch Shoals they arrive, and make ſuch a d—n'd Riot,
One can't take a Sup of one's Brimſtone in Quiet.

III.

Whole Armies come yonder, as I am alive,
Of Blacks and Mulattoes, from thundering *Clive*.
I wiſh his good King wou'd command him to *Britain*,
Or elſe this d———n'd Fuſs we ſhall never be quit on.

IV.

IV.

Ay!—rore till your Hearts ake, I'm deaf as the Tide,
Neither I or my Wherry, such Toil can abide ;
And if *Pluto* don't ease me of some o'this Pother,
Let his Devilship row, or else get him another.

V.

Odso !—a good Thought is just come in my Head,
To *Louis.* young *Mercury* strait shall be sped ;
His flat-bottom Boats sure he will not refuse,
He may very well spare, what he never can use.

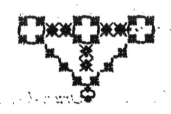

K   *Extem-*

Extempory EPIGRAM,

To Miss *Kitty F——n*, on seeing a pretty Chamber-maid of the Name of *Day*, at the Sign of the *Angel* at *Spinham Land*, on *Wednesday*, the 10th of *September*, 1760.

THE lesser Light
       To rule the Night,
Heaven gave to Man's revolving Years;
       Kit, hide thy Face,
       ('Tis no Disgrace)
Thou art but *Night* when *Day* appears.

Another, on the State of *Drury-lane Theatre*, 1760.

WHAT *M—k—n* too, and Daughter gone?
       Poor *Drury!*—Thou'lt be hard put to't,
Can *G——k* satisfy the Town?
       I hear he means to push a *Foot* *.

---

* *Push a Foot* is a common cant Phrase for running away; but in the above Epigram hints at an Engagement Mr. *G——k* was said to have made at that time with Mr. *Foote* for the ensuing Season.

The

The COACHMAN.

I.

A Long Fare, my Miftrefs, and to a Nick done,
For you fee that they have but this Moment
begun:
My Beafts are not fuch as are ey'd with a Grin,
I drive like a Devil, thro' Thick and thro' Thin:
With a Jayheu!——and a Lick at their Skin,
And away they do merrily fkip,
With Cits and Wits,
And dainty Bits,
With Beaux and Belles,
To *Sadler's Wells*:
O! fweet, fweet is the Smack of the Whip.

II.

As fure as I ftand here, in this fhabby Coat,
I was bred up at School, and learned Latin by rote,
My Dad would a Parfon fain had me a been,
But I was for driving thro' Thick and thro' Thin,
With a Jayheu!—and a Lick at their Skin,
And away do they merrily fkip,
With Wits and Cits,
And dainty Bits,
And Beaux and Belles,
To *Sadler's Wells*:
O! fweet, fweet is the Smack of the Whip.

My

III.

My Mother and I too were ftill at hot War,
For fhe faid I muft foon to the Court or the Bar;
But fay what fhe would, tho' I car'd not a Pin,
For I was for driving thro' Thick and thro' Thin;
   With a Jayheu, &c.

IV.

To Phyfic they urg'd me, and talk'd of a Wife,
But why hurt my own, or another Man's Life?
To fettle, my Mind by no means they could win,
For I was for driving thro' Thick and thro' Thin;
   With a Jayheu, &c.

V.

Fix your Point firft, faid Dad, and let Fate do the reft,
I'm glad that fo early you think for the beft,
For now a days few Men can hide a bare Skin,
Except 'tis by driving thro' Thick and thro' Thin;
   With a *John* go on—ait, Jayheu, fays *John*,
     And away flap-dab to his Grace,
       The Tye-wig and Bag,
       The Long-lawn and Shag,
       The Fops and the Fools,
       The knaves and the Tools,
    O fweet, fweet is the Hopes of a Place!

VI.

'Tis an Argument, Sir, that's too true, I reply'd,
But thy Dirt and my Dirt lie far enough wide;
Thine's bred in the Heart, mine but fticks to the Skin;
Excufe me for driving the Road that I'm in;
   With a Jayheu, and a Lick at their Skin, &c.

The

The SHEPHERD.

I.

T URN your Eye upon yonder fair Ground,
    And there a thatch'd Cot you may fee,
Which the Jefs'mine and Woodbines furround,
    And Fate hath beftow'd upon me

Variation.

Tho' thou haft loft a Lamb or Cow,
Smooth, O fmooth that Penfive brow;
Tho' thy Nymph prove falfly bent,
Come with me, and find Content ;
    For there fhe revels fair and free.

II.

'Tis the Sky-lark fhrill Note's all my Clock,
    My Care for my Kids and my Sheep ;
In my Dog, Crook, and Pipe lie my Stock,
    My Brook doth compofe me to Sleep.

Give, give, to thofe, their tinfell'd Toys,
    Thofe who know not Good to prize,
Thofe who dream of golden Joys,
    And wake to clafp what we defpife,
      Whom Health abandons, us to keep.

Tho'

III.

Tho' our Paint's the fresh air of the Morn,
 Our Wash the pearl Dew of the Sky;
Tho' no Silks do our Lasses adorn,
 Their Bloom the Town-dames doth defy.

Away then, Truth, and tell the Cause;
 Nor Hate, nor Pride, we Shepherds feel;
Of Love and Mirth we keep the Laws;
 Sweet Peace attends our ev'ry Meal,
  And stops all Harm from sliding by.

A

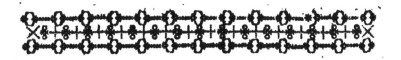

A *Loyal* BALLAD.

I.

YE Free-born of Britain, rejoice ye, rejoice,
Shout, fhout, O ye Millions, as 'twere with a
    Voice,
    Till the clamorous Croud
    Be fo joyoufly loud,
    That great *Lewis* the proud,
That Monarch of Shadows, be fcar'd at our Joys;
    When at length from his Fear,
    He recovers, and dare
To demand from what Quarter the Noife,
    Then O fay, fay, ye Slaves,
    From the Sons of the Waves,
From the brave, from the brave, from the brave *Britifh* Boys.
    Brave *Britifh* Boys,
    Brave *Britifh* Boys,
From the brave, from the brave, from the brave *Britifh* Boys.

                    II.

II.

Then tell to your Tyrant, O tell him the Cause;
Say our Church and our Wealth, our Freedom and Laws,
    Have been so preferr'd
    By King *George the Third*,
    With Zeal we are stirr'd
His Rights to protect, and his Honour to raise;
    And that therefore we'll roar
    On the Protestant Shore,
Till we strain all our Throats to his Praise;
    To the Monarch 'tis due,
    To our Countryman too;
He's our first *English* King, for these many fair Days;
    Many fair Days,
    Many fair Days,
He's our first *English* King, for these many fair Days.

A New

A BALLAD.

I.

WHY turn thofe damafk Rofes pale?
O fee young *Jenny* trips the Vale!
Their Red the neighb'ring Lillies wear,
They blufh with Envy, fhe's fo fair.

II.

The Sun, bright Ruler of the Day,
Stops fhort his Courfers on their Way;
Yet fcarce a Minute dare he gaze,
On her more potent, piercing Rays.

III.

No King can copy *Jenny's* Grace,
No Queen e'er boafted fuch a Face;
But hark, fhe warbles, feather'd Choir,
Ye and Angels muft admire.

IV.

'Mongft matchlefs Beauties, Charms fhe wears,
Shall dare the rougheft Shock of Years;
As free from vicious Thoughts as Deeds,
And artlefs as the Lambs fhe feeds.

V.

V.

With one from all the World beside,
The fair referv'd one deigns to hide;
To all but him as Darknefs blind,
Happieft he of human Kind.

VI.

Each Morn they rife at Peep o' Dawn,
To chafe the Lev'ret o'er the Lawn,
To hook the Fifh, to fearch the Neft.
Produce me Courts a Pair fo bleft.

A BALLAD.

I.

B Y a Prince *Britiſh* born we are ſway'd,
    With a Stateſman all-wiſe at our Helm ;
Riſe Liberty, Honour, and Trade,
    The Props of this fortunate Realm.

II.

'er a ſcandalous Train of foul Deeds,
    Religion, fair Victor, I ſee ;
nd wou'd ſmile, but my poor Boſom bleeds :
    All, all can be happy but me !

III.

Breath, yet oh Time ! — yet, oh ! hence
    I am torn with theſe teat-redn'd Eyes :
fight againſt Nature and Senſe
    A Skirmiſh that ſtaggers the Wiſe.

IV.

Tis not that I go for my King,
    One Pang yet hath enter'd my Heart ;
lut *Sally !*———there breaks every String !
    Ah *Sally !* I die when we part.

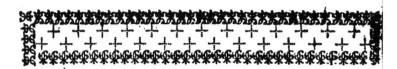

A PROLOGUE,

Spoken by Miſs *Pitt*, at the Theatre *Jacob's Well*, on *Wedneſday* the 19th of *Auguſt*, 1761; in Recommendation of a young Actreſs to the Protection of the Public.

THE tragic Muſe, in glittering Pomp array'd,
Join'd by her blooming Siſter, lovely Maid!
With Harmony and Dance, and decent Jeſt,
Thro' me thus hail their Patrons of the Weſt.

To ſome grave Ears 'tis Death to name a Play;
Too dull to mend, ſuch leave I to their Way,
And thus addreſs the Wiſe, the Learn'd, the Gay.
To agitate the generous Mind with Scorn
Of tyrant Loads, diſguſtful to be borne;
Traitors to ſcourge, and Pride and lawleſs Sway,
And ſuch who dare their native Land betray,
To ſtigmatize the Coward, fix the Blot,
On Men whoſe Crimes ſhou'd never be forgot:
To paint Love's Perjuries, till the Heart ſincere
Heaves with fond Sobs, and trickling falls the Tear;
To puniſh Vice, to ſtem Corruption's Tide,
Howe'er it be adorn'd or dignify'd;
True Merit to reward, on any Ground,
Whether in Temple, Court, or Hamlet found;

Such

Such shou'd be all Mens Study, such their Care,
So wills *Melpomene* ;———so speaks the PLAYER.
But if too formal shou'd the Maid appear,
In bounds her sprightly Sister, light as Air !
Whose Paths, tho' pleasanter they seem to wind,
Alike to Good excite each well-turn'd Mind.
From Misers, Jilts, Reformers, Fribbles, Bucks,
Jobbers and Gulls, the motly Mask she plucks.
Of Mates morose she blabs ; of much wrong'd Spouses;
Of boozing 'Squires, their Kennels and their Houses ;
Of Wives provok'd, and careless Husbands tells,
And peeps in ev'ry Nook where Folly dwells.
Exposes all her Tribe to open Weather,
And fairly shews you who and who's together.

Late (as I dream't) Fame whisper'd in my Ear,
Such are the Walks design'd for you, my Dear :
The Scepter, Ermine, Dagger, and the Bowl,
Early reject; be thine to chear the Soul
With dimpl'd Smiles, quick Repartee and Jest,
To Nature stick, and leave to me the Rest.
Be emulous to please a generous Town,
That saw thy Dawn, and mark'd thee for it's own.
Young as I am, and unexperienc'd, yet
I can but promise, and enhance the Debt :
Will ye then wait with Patience till you see
How truly grateful I shall strive to be,
Till from your kindly Warmth I by degrees
Ripen to Worth perhaps, perhaps to please ?
O ! still regard me with those Looks so mild,
And for the Parent's Sake indulge the Child.

A

A BALLAD.

Sung by Mrs. *Dennis* at *Sadler's Wells*.

I.

BY the Light of the Moon t'other Ev'ning I stray'd
   A Mile by the Side o'the Brook;
   When *Roger* stept up with, how do you, fair
     Maid?
    I peevishly answer'd, go look—go look—
       I peevishly answer'd, go look.

II.

Nay, nay, he reply'd, why so angry with me?
   I know you meet *Robin* the Cook;
It may be you now are a waiting for he.
   In Passion I answer'd, go look—go look—
      In Passion I answer'd, go look.

III.

Quoth he, you love Music, I've heard them to say;
   And out he an Instrument took;——
D'ye think, said he, *Bob* or I better can play?
   I answer'd him, Fellow, go look—go look—
      I answer'd him, Fellow go look.

IV.

IV.

But refolute grown, he feiz'd faft o'my Hand,
 And forc'd me fit down in the Nook;
And Sweet, faid he, tell me what Tunes you command.
 You Puppy, I anfwer'd, go look—go look—
    You Puppy, I anfwer'd, go look.

V.

But foon, with his Flute, he fo ravifh'd my Heart,
 That I never dreamt more of the Cook;
And thofe who imagine I've told but a Part,
 For the reft of the Story may look—may look—
    For the reft of the Story may look.

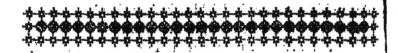

A Loyal SONG.

Sung by Mr. *Green* at *Sadler's Wells.*

I.

OUR Glory renown'd on the Ocean and Shore,
 To Ages, for aye, shall be told;
Hawke, Howe and *Boscawen, Wolf, Amherst* and
 Moor,
 In the Lift of fair Fame be inroll'd.
In Praise of such Leaders, then open your Throats,
 And laugh at the *French,*
 Laugh at the *French,*
Laugh at the *French,* and their flat-bottom'd Boats.

II.

While *Barrington* sweft off the Table *Baf'terre,*
 At *Minden* we got the odd Trick;
Shew'd *Conflans* a Trump or two, made him look queer,
 And won all they had at *Quebec.*
Then sing and be jolly, Boys, open your Throats,
 And laugh at the *French,*
 Laugh at the *French,*
Laugh at the *French,* a n d their flat-bottom'd Boats.

III.

We're ignorant what may betide the new Year,
    But certain of this we are all ;——
Her Courfe how fhe will let kind Providence fteer ;
    For Freedom we fight, and we'll fall.——
For King *George*, and Prince *George*, then open your Throats,
        And laugh at the *French*,
        Laugh at the *French* ;——
Laugh at the *French*, and their flat-bottom'd Boats.

IV.

Like Greyhounds half ftarv'd they fquint at our Food,
    And fain from our Beef wou'd be fed ;
Ye're welcome, Monfieurs, if you'll wade to't in Blood ;
    I fee you are far better bred.——
Poltroons !——how they run !——then open your Throats,
        And laugh at the *French*,
        Laugh at the *French* !
Laugh at the *French*, and their flat-bottom'd Boats.

L   *A*

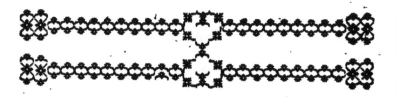

A SONG.

TO the Wood Robin Red Breaſt is flown,
 The Dairy he viſits no more;
 The Violets and Cowſlips are blown,
  The Cuckoo's heard e'ery Field o'er.

Thro' the Grove ſwells the Blackbird's ſtrong Note,
 In Concert with ſofter ton'd Thruſh;
The Lark ſtretches wide his ſhrill Throat,
 And Linnets are heard on each Buſh.

The Hawthorns are powder'd with May,
 The Meadows array'd are in Green,
The Ewes, with their Lambs, are at Play;
 Ah, Nature! how lovely each Scene!

Yet, alas! what the Beauties of Spring
 For my Eaſe, ah, too ſoon are they come;
They bring the Commands of the King,
 To march after Bagpipe and Drum.

And

And *Donald*, my Darling, muſt go ;
  It may be for ever we part ;
But when that ſad Tale I ſhall know,
  That Moment breaks *Annice*'s Heart.

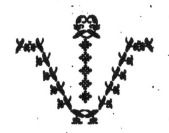

The

The *Loyal* FARMER,

Sung by Mr. *Andrews,* and others, at *Sadler's Wells.*

I.

NOW the Cuckoo, from Climate remote,
    Returns to our neighbouring Groves;
And the Ificles wat'ry Coat,
    Hath funk from the Perch of the Doves.
By the Beams of the Sun will we warm us;
Old Beer, Songs and Dances, fhall charm us;
    At *Eafter* what Evil can harm us?
Each light as a Fawn or a Bird,
    Jolly Neighbours fet to't,
    With Heart, Hand and Foot;
Here's a Brufher to *George* the Third.

                    Drinks.

II.

II.

Again thro' the Air,
Soft Warblers appear;
No longer pent up are the Bees:
The sweet Nightingale
Is return'd to the Vale,
And the Buds are restor'd to the Trees.——
By the Beams of the Sun will we warm us,
Old Beer, Songs and Dances shall charm us;
At *Easter* what Evil can harm us?
Each light as a Fawn or a Bird;
Jolly Neighbours set to't,
With Heart, Hand and Foot;
To the Mother of *George* the Third.

Drinks.

III.

Warm Sillabub now,
Milk'd under the Cow;
And Cream Cheese the Dairy supplies;
At Foot of each Oak,
We frisk it, and joke,
And Love as we live, without Lies.——
By the Beams of the Sun will we warm us,
Old Beer, Songs and Dances shall charm us;
At *Easter* what Evil can harm us?
Each light as a Fawn or a Bird;
Jolly Neighbours set to't,
With Heart, Hand and Foot;
To the Brother of *George* the Third.

Drinks.

IV.

IV.

The Corn's above Ground,
So ftrike up a Round ;
At *Eafter* fuch ftill be our Guife ;
And this we can do,
All Holidays too ;
Becaufe we are merry and wife.
By the Beams of the Sun will we warm us,
Old Beer, Songs and Dances fhall charm us ;
At *Eafter* what Evil can harm us ?
Each light as a Fawn or a Bird ;
Jolly Neighbours fet to't,
With Heart, Hand and Foot ;
Great Britain and *George* the Third,

Drinks.

Grand Chorus of Farmers and their Wives, at the laft
Line of each Verfe.

An

An Albion **S O N G.**

I.

WHEN *England*'s free Scepter *Elizabeth* fway'd,
Then profper'd our Armies, then flourifh'd our
Trade.
The *Frenchmen* then fwagger'd, but fwagger'd in vain,
And bang came the thund'ring *Armado* of *Spain.*
Oh, how did the mighty *Invincible*'s jeer ;
But fhe fent the Don back with a Flea in his Ear:
And *George*, our young Monarch, the Third of that Name,
Her Equal in Spirit fhall equal her Fame.

II.

'Gainft *Howard* and *Raleigh, Frobifher* and *Drake,*
Yorke, Anfon, Hawke, Saunders, and *Pococke,* we ftake ;
For *Effex* and *Cecil* we've *Granby* and *Pitt* ;
And *Britain*, as ufual, triumphant fhall fit ;
Her Soldiers and Sailors, commanded aright,
Are able and eager as ever to fight,
That *George* their young Monarch, the Third of that Name,
As gallant in Spirit, be equal in Fame.

III.

The hardy bold *Albions* are still what they were,
Th' Assertors of Right, the Contemners of Fear.
When Country and King, and Religion invoke,
Like their Bull Dogs they fight, and they stand like their
      Oak.
Then *Gallia*, your haughty Bravados, have done;
Our Annals can shew what our Princes have won.
And *George*, our young Monarch, the Third of that Name,
Their equal in Spirit, shall equal their Fame.

IV.

At *Agincourt*, *Cressey*, *Anjou* and *Poictiers*,
Our *Henrys* and *Edwards* once cow'd ye with Fears;
The Force of those Leaders, forget if ye can,
With *Ramilies*, *Blenbeim*, brave *Marlbro'* and *Anne*:
Late, *Minden*, *Quebec*, *Senegal* and *Goree*;
And say, who shou'd laugh then? is't you, Sirs, or we?
Great *George*, our young Monarch, the Third of that Name,
Shall conquer what's left ye, and fix his fair Fame.

In Honour of the King of Pruffia.

A CANTATA.

RECITATIVE.

THE thick'ning Bands in terrible Array,
Like baneful Locufts fpread the hoftile Plain ;
As a foul Blight, the num'rous Vermin fwarm'd,
And blafted all the Beauties of the Year.

AIR.

In queft of royal Game,
The favage Hunters came ;
Inglorious were the Fame,
Had they obtain'd the Fight !

CHORUS.

But what are Millions 'gainft the Rod
Of an incens'd avenging God !
In vain proud Priefts to paltry Idols fing ;
The God of Gods is with the *Pruffian* King.

RECIT.

RECIT.

The Scourge of foul Idolaters behold,
Frederick the juft, the clement Hero, fee!—
Smiling, ferene amidft furrounding Storms,
Whilft well-train'd Chiefs, attend his lov'd Commands.

AIR.

And now flies the Ball ;
See, they bleed !——fee they fall!——
The Steeds how they curvet and bound ;——
Hark, the terrible Roar !——
See a Deluge of Gore.——
They flee, and the King keeps the Ground.
Huzza! Huzza!
They flee, and the King keeps the Ground.

RECIT.

Perfidious *France*, and *Hungary*'s cruel Queen,
With all the Aid of their combin'd Allies,
Now find their fubtle Wiles of flender Force,
Againft a Sovereign Piety protects.——

AIR.

A I R.

Their vaſt Battalions, ſee !
How ſhamefully they flee,
   Before his rapid Arm ;
Who plotted his Diſgrace,
Now dare not view his Face ;
   So awful Virtues charm.

C H O R U S.

Nations unborn his wond'rous Acts ſhall ſing,
And Worlds on Worlds adore the *Pruſſian* King.

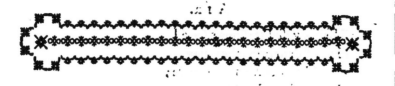

A SONG.

I.

FAREWEL lovely Queen of Cares,
In vain thy Son his Bow prepares;
Too lazy *Paphos*, from thy Shore
I fly; and truft thy Nymphs no more.———

II.

A deadly Poifon lurks unfeen
In Breaft fo white, in Eye fo keen;
By ftormy Tempefts rather whirl'd,
I court the Wave;———the Sail's unfurl'd.

III.

Britannia's free-born Sons to fave,
From thofe who wou'd the World enflave;
My trufty Blade fhall foon be drawn,
And *Frenchmen's* Blood befmear the Lawn.

IV.

IV.

Before our King shall lose his Right,
We'll crowd with *French* the Realms of Night ;
In spite of Saints, ten thousand Score,
The D———l, Pope, and *Pompadour*.

V.

'Till haughty *Louis*, Cap in Hand,
Gives all we ask, by Sea and Land ;
Our roaring Cannons shall not cease ;
They best can fix the Terms of Peace.

AN-

ANOTHER.

I.

AS I at *Fanny*'s, t'other Day,
Sat gazing of my Soul away;
She afk'd a Knife, I fetch'd a Chair;
Good Lord! what Fools we Lovers are.——

II.

She faid, too high her Goldfinch hung;
I curft the Bird, but bleft her Tongue.
My Anfwer made her laugh and ftare;
Good Lord! what Fools we Lovers are.——

III.

She told me plainly I was mad;
And troth, if 'twere fo, I'd be glad;
For now I pine and droop with Care;
Good Lord! what Fools we Lovers are.——

IV.

IV.

I mope and lounge about ● Houſe,
And hate e'en Dog, or Cat, or Mouſe,
That chance in *Fanny*'s Face to leer.
Good Lord! what Fools we Lovers are.

V.

O *Fanny*! eaſe my raging Pain!
O bind me with the Marriage Chain.
When will you name the Day, my Dear?—
O Lord! what Fools we Lovers are.

A Pastoral S O N G,

Introduced in the Character of a Hay-maker in
Harlequin Deserter.

The Music by Mr. *Pattersal.*

I.

WHILE Southern Breezes bless the Morn,
And fan the Dew from off the Thorn;
And soaring Larks, with early Notes,
To hail the Day, retune their Throats,
  Full of Play,
  Blithe as May,
We trip to make the new mown Hay.——

II.

Full lightly skim we o'er the Mead,
With Cowslips and with Dazies spread;
Primroses, Violets, white and blue,
And Butterflowers of golden Hue,
   Bright and gay,
   Sweet as they,
Appear our Girls amongst the Hay.

II

Then who more happy are than we?
Or who can boaſt a Life ſo free?
We know no Guile, we know no Pain;
We laugh at Sorrow; Care diſdain.——
                    Kiſs and play,
                    Homage pay,
To Love on Altars made with Hay.

IV.

Yet think not, Friends, by what we ſing,
We mean to ſkulk from *George* the King;
For ſhou'd the Foe his Realms invade,
We'd quit the Rake, and wield the Blade.
                    Give up Play,
                    French to ſlay;
And leave the Girls to make the Hay.

M

***

A SONG.

I.

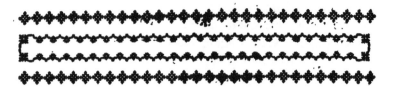AY, jeer ye not, Sisters, by Love unbetray'd,
But pity a fond, yet an innocent Maid ;
I step'd but with *Johnny* to yonder Hedge-row ;
And which of ye all, pray, wou'd not have done so ?——

II.

If with him, he said, to the Coppice I'd stray,
He'd gather me Violets, and Bloom of the *May* ;
Then kiss'd me so sweetly, I cou'd not but go ;
And which of you all, pray, had answer'd him, No ?

III.

At the Foot of a wide swelling Oak we reclin'd ;
I lean'd on his Breast while he whisper'd his Mind ;
His Offer was Marriage, I cou'dn't say, No ;
Pray which of ye all is't that wou'd have done so ?——

IV.

IV.

As the Ivy around this ftout Oak doth entwine,
So, Sweeting, faid he, thou muft do when thou'rt mine;
Then clafp'd me clofe to him,—I begg'd I might go;
But he prefs'd me ftill clofer, and cry'd, my Dear, No.—

V.

Alas, gentle *Johnny!* fweet *Johnny!* I faid,
Remember your Promife, nor hurt a poor Maid;
Confider my Virtue, and pray let me go;
But he kifs'd me ftill warmer, and cry'd, my Dear, No.

VI.

I ever thought *Johnny* as mild as the Dove;
How weak is the Heart that gives Sanction to Love?
Yet he fwears that To-morrow to Church he will go;
He fhall ne'er get me out again till he does fo.

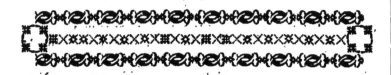

A Drinking SONG.

Sung by Mr. *Atkins*.

I.

CUPID, you fneaking young Dog, I defpife you,
Fly from this Spot—like a Friend I advife you;
Pox o'your Quiver, you Fool, we don't fear it;
We are defended by Punch, Wine, and Claret.
Sing, Huzza, be jolly, be frolickfome here,
We've nothing to think of, fo nothing to fear.

II.

He that is heavily laden with Sorrow,
Adds to the Burden by Thoughts of To-morrow.
Reafon and Gravity buckle behind ye,
Tricks of the Sophifters only to blind ye.——
   Sing, Huzza, be jolly, &c.
   We've nothing to think of, &c.

III.

III.

Look at our Motto there, *Nunc eſt Bibendum* ;
Thoſe that are ſick, why the Bottle muſt mend 'em ;
He that's a Bankrupt; why let him heed nought on't ;
This is the Centre to bury the Thought on't.——
   Sing, Huzza, be jolly, *&c.*
   We've nothing to think of, *&c.*

IV.

Come, charge for a Toaſt now, my Choice, merry Souls ;
Good Lord! how I love to ſee Bumpers and Bowls !——
Here's a Health to King *George* the Third e're I depart,
And he that won't pledge me's a Dog in his Heart.
   Sing, Huzza, be jolly, *&c.*
   We've nothing to think of, *&c.*

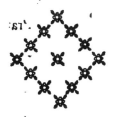

     The

The Prudent Fair.

A SONG.

I.

THAT ferious Look,—that penfive Air,
Reafon whifpers, Maid beware!
You pine with Love;———you fay you'll die.
You have Art———but Virtue I.

II.

My Face, my Shape, my fimple Lays,
Attract, you fwear, your warmeft Praife.
Ruin lurks in either Eye;
Thou haft Art———but Virtue I.

III.

Gentle Wanton tempt me not;
To Grove's Recefs, or gloomy Grot;
I've juft the Skill to Vice defy;
Art thou haft———but Virtue I.

IV.

IV.

Ever public be our Walk;
If of Love, of Marriage talk,
Colour changes, I defcry;
Faithlefs Youth!————for aye good bye.

The

The Invitation to Sadler's Wells,

On their Opening, in 1759.

Sung by Mr. *Atkins*.

I.

YE wise ones abandon the Cynical Rules,
 Insipid, and fit but for Friery Cells!
The nauseous dry Food of pedantical Fools.
 Come, come ye away to *Sadler's Wells* ;
And revel——drink, and dance, and buss,
And keep your Holidays with us.

II.

Ye Lads, and ye Lasses, why waste ye your Prime ?
 Why languid in Health, and in Vigour why pine ?
Why wou'd you affront your poor old Daddy Time ?
 Who loves at his Heart the fat God of the Vine.
Then revel——drink, and dance and buss,
And keep your Holidays with us.

III.

III.

With fprightly Variety, 'tis that we mean,
   To hit off the Taftes of all Sorts and Degrees ;
With moral, and frolic, and gay gilded Scene,
   And every Amufement that's likely to pleafe.
Then revel——drink, and dance, and bufs,
And keep your Holidays with us.

IV.

See, fee the fair Nymph* all fufpended in Air ;
   See *Harlequin* neat, and the blundering Clown ;
See the Graces, the Loves, and the Wood-nymphs appear ;
   No Coft fhall be fpar'd to give Joy to the Town.
Then revel——drink, and dance, and bufs,
And keep your Holidays with us.

* Mifs *Wilkinfon.*

For

For the KING's Birth-Day, 1761.

RECITATIVE.

WITH Glee unuſual *Phœbus* mounts his Car,
 Before him ſkims the Goddeſs, ſpotleſs
  Fame;
 She ſounds the natal Day of *George* the
  Third,
 And cluſt'ring Subjects hail their much-
  lov'd King.

AIR.

Care avaunt the regal Brow,
Fate preſerve it, mild as now ;————
Ne'er, O Time, a Thought impart,
From *Dolour's* Cell to *George's* Heart;
But keep it ſtill in pleaſant Tune,
The royal Roſe of fragrant *June.*

 Come, let's make the Welkin ring
With, Live great *George!* Long live the King!
Let's raiſe the Voice, and touch the String;
And ſtill remember whilſt we ſing,
A *Briton* born is *Britain's* King.————

RECIT.

R E C I T.

To Blood and Slaughter, not by Madnefs ftirr'd,
As once the hot brain'd *Macedonian* Youth ;
But Freedom to fecure, fair Faith and Truth.
Great *George*'s Thunder awes the Vaffal World.

A I R.

But foon fhall fair Peace come again,
   The richeft of Diadems worn ;
Our Trade then fhall flourifh amain,
   And our Youth be as gay as the Morn.

And in the mean while will we drink, roar and fing ;
   The Cannon fhall play, and the Bonfires blaze ;
'Tis the Birth-day of *George* the Third, *England*'s King.
     May Heaven direct him,
     Enfold, and protect him ;
And fend him a Reign made of all happy Days.

A Hunting SONG.

RECITATIVE.

THE high-pois'd Lark, salutes the opening Dawn;
The dripping Cowslips rear their dewy Heads;
Across the Copse the ruddy Milkmaid chants,
And *Phœbus* tints with Gold his *Richmond* Hill.

AIR.

With well scented Hounds, and with jolly-ton'd Horn,
We'll rouse the proud Stag with the first of the Morn.
See, see from the Covert, how stoutly he springs:
Hark! hark! the Pack opens ;—'tis Music for Kings.
With Scorn and Disdain how he snuffs up the Wind,
He leaps the Park Wall, and he throws us behind.
No more he perceives us, gets rid of his Pain ;
Tan ta ra, says Eccho !——They're with you again.

Thro'

Thro' Woodlands then he leads the Sweep,
He fords the *Thames*, he climbs the Steep ;
The Brow he gains,————he ftops,————he turns,
He fears,————he pants————he chills————he burns !

To the Herd then he fcowers amain ;
His Suit to the Herd proves in vain ;
He faints !————he drops !————the Huntfman cries
Dead ! dead ! ware Haunch !————he dies, he dies.

A

A BACCHANALIAN SONG.

COME bind my Brows, ye Wood-nymphs fair,
    With Ivy Wreaths come bind my Brows ;
Hence Grief and Woe, and Pain and Care,
    To *Bacchus* I devote my Vows.————
        Dull *Cynic* Rules,
        Are fit for Tools ;
Let thofe digeft the Food who can :
        But Love and Wine
        Shall ftill be mine ;
O let me laugh out all my Span.

No Wounds, O Love, e'er let me feel,
    But fuch as fpring from Eyes and Shapes ;
A Curfe on thofe that come by Steel ;
    I hate all Blood, but Blood of Grapes.

        Then fill up high
        The Bowl, that I
May drink and laugh at Fools of Senfe.
        Why need we fear
        To want next Year ;
'Twill be all one a Hundred hence.

EPIGRAM,

On the Death of Mr. *Edward Berry*, late of *Drury Lane* Theatre.

W

HEN Heaven sent Death honest *Ned* to en-
gage,
He knock'd at the Door, but was told in a
Rage,
That he cou'dn't get up ;—*Ned* took him for *Page* † :
Death popp'd in his Head with a Grin, and reply'd,
Your Tragedy, Comedy, Farce throw aside ;
It is now to rehearse before *Jove* you're requir'd :
I've been perfect these twelve Years, said *Ned*, and expir'd.

---

† The Porter of the House, a principal Part of whose Business
it is to summon the Performers every Morning to the Rehearsal.

TOTTERDOWN-HILL:

A SONG.

I.

AT *Totterdown-hill* there dwelt an old Pair,
And it may be they dwell there ftill;
Much Riches indeed didn't fall to their Share,
They kept a fmall Farm and a Mill.

II.

But fully content with what they did get,
They knew nought of Guile or of Arts;
One Daughter they had, her Name it was *Bet*,
And fhe was the Joy of their Hearts.

III.

Nut-brown were her Locks, her Shape it was ftrait,
Her Eyes were as black as a Sloe,
Her Teeth were milk-white, full fmart was her Gait,
And as fleek was her Skin as a Doe.

IV.

IV.

All dark were the Clouds, and the Rain it did pour,
    No Bit of true Blue cou'd be fpy'd;
A Child numb'd with Cold came and knock'd at the Door,
    It's Mam it had loft, and it cry'd.

V.

Young *Bet* was as mild as a Morn of fweet *May*,
    The Babe fhe hugg'd clofe to her Breaft;
She chaf'd him all o'er, and he fmil'd as he lay,
    She cuddl'd and lull'd him to Reft.

VI.

But who do you think was this very fine Prize?
    Why, Love, the young Mafter of Arts:
As foon as he wak'd he fhook off his Difguife,
    And fhew'd her his Wings and his Darts.

VII.

Quoth he, I am *Cupid*, but be not afraid,
    Tho' all I make fhake at my Will;
So good and fo kind is your Heart, my fair Maid,
    No Harm fhall you feel from my Skill.

VIII.

My Mother ne'er dealt with more Fondnefs by me;
    As fuch I fhall look on you ftill:
Take my Bow and my Darts, and be greater than fhe,
    The *Venus* of *Totterdown-hill.*

A S O N G.

I.

I N yon Grot my Lover lies,
Sleep has clos'd his godlike Eyes;
Weary'd with the blood-ftain'd Chace,
Let him reft a little Space.
Ye whom Chance may bring that way,
Soft, O foft ye tread, I pray;
Fall not rude your ruftic Feet,
For there lies all that's good and great.

II.

Mild as is the Morning Sun,
Fond as is the Turtle Dove,
Fleet as Ball from loaded Gun,
Certain as the Bolt of *Jove*.
Now tell, and tell true, ye Nymphs of the Plain,
Shou'd fuch a Man love, could you love him again?
If you cou'd then be tender, and do not me blame,
Love ever hath had the Advantage of Fame.

The

The Introductory Plan of the Pantomime called *Harlequin Deferter*; as it was originally intended to have been performed at *Sadler's Wells*; but could only in part be executed, on account of the violent Indisposition of one of the principal Performers.

On the Curtain's rising, a Recruiting Sergeant, with Corporal, Drum, and Mob following : Harlequin in the Character of a Farmer's Servant ; the Farmer's Son, and Columbine amongst them.

Sergeant sings.

COME, Volunteers, come
  To the Head of the Drum,
  And all you can muster along with you bring ;
  Leave Fathers and Mothers,
   And Sisters and Brothers,
Nor think of a Duty, but that to your King.

  Thou'rt active young Neighbour, *(To Harlequin.*
  Then throw off thy Labour,
And swop thy base Pillow for Bed of Renown ;
  Dick, *Harry*, and *Hugh*, *(To the Countrymen.*
  Won't ye do so too?
A Guinea I'll give, ye do see !—and a Crown,

        Good

Good Linen and Cloaths,
With Hats, Shoes and Hose,
For a Gentleman Soldier fit every Thing;
To my Quarters then come,
And of Brandy and Rum
Swig till your Belly's full: God save the King.

(Drum beats.

Harlequin sings.

Serjeant, thou'rt an honest Fellow,
Blood let's go, and get us mellow;
I do loike a Life so funny,
Gi's thy Hond,—I'll take the Money:
Who a Pleague wud vollow ploughing.
Reap and thresh and go to mowing?
When he might be Pleasure teaking,
Drinking, dancing, rawring, reaking.
I do loike a loife so funny,
Gi's thy Hond, I'll teake the Money.

Tol de rol.

As Harlequin is receiving the Money, Columbine advances
and sings.

Stop, stop, you foolish Ninny,
Give him back his paltry Guinea,
   Thou'lt repent it by and by;   (To Harlequin.
What! my sapskull Brother too,
Prythee Hodge be quiet, do,
   I'll vetch Feyther, let me die.

   Tho' I gave, the other Day, (To Harlequin, crying.
To Dick, a Bowl of Curds and Whey,
It was; my Heart, indeed but Play;
Therefore do not hence away.

Roger

Roger sings.

Of Feyther pray who be avroid,
  Or who be avroid of Moother;
I'll lift with the Sarjeant, you Jade,
  As zure as that I am thy Brother.

The Devil uh bides in the Wench,
  Daunt we go for King *George* our Defender,
To keep out the damnable *French*,
  The Papifts, and bloody Pretender?

Enter Farmer and sings.

Thowts mifgove me when I mift'n!
Sarjant, Sarjant, daun'tee lift un :
Haft uh don't ?—Then here's the Money,
To difcharge the fimple Tony.
                         (*Returns the Money to the Sarjant.*

Happy for him that they're parted,
E're yon Dog had got him carted ;   (*Pointing to Harlequin.*
Deed of his I will not alter,
Shot perhaps may fave the Halter.
                         (*Exeunt Father and Son.*

Columbine advances and sings.

Why then, my dear Father and Mother, adieu!
My Cot and my Flock I'll abandon for you;
To march with my Harley fhall ftill be my Pride,
And I'll fleep, and I'll walk, and I'll fight by thy Side.

N 3   *Harlequin*

Harlequin sings.

Now lovely, charming, faithful Dear,
It is not safe to loiter here :
Already we have stay'd too late,
I'll meet you at your Quarters strait.   (*To the Sergeant.*

Sergeant.

Duke *William*'s Head without the Gate.
                    Exeunt separately, Drum beating.

During the Course of the Entertainment, Harlequin, having deserted from his Regiment, is discovered at a Tavern with Columbine, and made Prisoner by the Sergeant.

Sergeant sings.

Run-away Dog! have I caught you?
      You and your trolloping Beauty?
Better Things soon shall be taught you,
      Hand-cuff, and drag him to Duty.

As the Soldiers are about to hand-cuff him, Colombine beckons the Sergeant, and shews a Purse; on which the Sergeant sends off the Men, takes the Purse from her, and sings.

Heartily thank you, my Dear,
      Sorry so far that we jested ;
Harly, my Lad, you are clear,
      You have n't as yet been attested.
                    (*Harlequin and Colombine go off.*

Sergeant sings.

Is there a Man you can bring,
   Wou'dn't do this for the Pelf, Sir?   *(Shakes the Purse.*
One I hold tight for the King,
   Three I let go for myself, Sir.
            Exit singing Tol, tol, tol, &c·

                             A

A *Loyal* SONG.

I.

O Peace with the *Frenchmen*, were I to direct,
But bang 'till you've bang'd them to proper
Respect.
    To the Gates of *Verfailles* should our Cannon
    advance,
And the Grenadier's March shou'd frighten all *France.*
    This *British* Boys wou'd do with Glee,
    For royal *George* and Liberty,
    George the Third and Liberty.
    Come fill your Glasses—drink with me,
    The Words are *George* and Liberty.

II.

Let's pay 'em and flay 'em on Land and on Main,
We have, my Lads, often, and why not again?
Their *Creffy* and *Poictiers* and *Agincourt* shew
What *Britons*, when pitted with *Frenchmen*, can do.
    To Action then, brave Boys, with Glee,
    For royal *George* and Liberty, *&c.*

III.

How oft we've been cheated by Art and Chicane,
But now we can tell 'em such efforts are vain :
That Feuds are deſtroy'd, and that Party's a Joke,
And all *England* united, as not to be broke.
    But one and all will fight with Glee,
    For royal *George* and Liberty, *&c.*

IV.

Whene'er the King pleaſes to ſay do it now,
Hawke, *Saunders* and *Pocock*, brave *Granby* and *Howe*,
Shall burn, ſink, and plunder, and lower their Notes,
In ſpite of Pope, Devil, and flat-bottom Boats.
    To Deeds like theſe they'd go with Glee,
    For royal *George* and Liberty, *&c.*

V.

See our Rocks that defend us and taunt 'em with Scorn;
See our prudent young Monarch, an *Engliſhman* born ;
See, of Traytors regardleſs, he ſmiles on his Throne,
For he knows that each Heart in his Kingdom's his own.
    And that each Arm would ſtrike with Glee,
    For royal *George* and Liberty, *&c.*

I

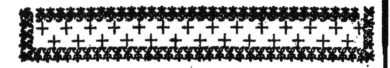

The GOOD FELLOW.

A SONG.

I.

DISTANT fly thee, carping Care,
 From the Spot where I do dwell ;——
 Rigid Mortals come not there ;
  Frowns begone to Hermit Cell.——
But let me live the Life of Souls,
 With Love, and Laugh, and flowing Bowls:

II.

Miser, with thy paltry Pelf,
 I give 'gainst thee my Hate its Scope ;
Wretch, that liv'st but for thyself,
 With Heart of Rust that cannot ope.——
  Fly, Bird of Night, from Sun and Souls,
  That love and laugh o'er flowing Bowls.

III.

III.

Who can let the Penfive go,
    Or the Eye that drops a Tear;
And not weed their Minds of Woe,
    May not dare to peep in here.————
      Who can't be Friends can ne'er be Souls,
      Nor e'er fhall quaff our flowing Bowls.————

IV.

Joys on Joys, O let me tafte;
    Health and Mirth, dwell in my Gate;
Whilft with Eafe my Sand doft wafte,
    Whilft I blefs the Book of Fate.————
      That let's me live the Life of Souls,
      With Love and Laugh, and flowing Bowls.

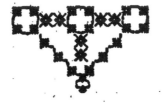

A SONG.

I.

O Reaſon, ye Fair-Ones, aſſert your Pretence,
Nor hearken to Language beneath common
    Senſe:
When Angels Men call ye, and Homage wou'd
    pay,
If you credit the Tale, you're as faulty as they.—

II.

Ten thouſand gay Scenes are preſented to View,
Ten thouſand Oaths ſworn, but not one of them true:
Such Paſſions, O heed not, unleſs to deride,
Leſt a Victim you fall to an ill-grounded Pride.

III.

Prefer ye the Dictates of Virtue to Sound,
True Bleſſings can ne'er without Goodneſs be found:
Leave Folly and Faſhion, Miſguiders of Youth,
And ſtick to their Oppoſites, Freedom and Truth.

A

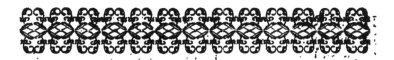

A SONG,

Sung by Mr. *Lowe* at *Vauxhall.*

I.

ON the white Clifts of *Albion*, fee Fame where fhe ftands,
And her fhrill fwelling Notes reach the neighbouring Lands.
Of the Natives free born, and their Conquefts, fhe fings:
The happieft of Men, with the greateft of Kings.——

II.

George the Third fhe proclaims, his vaft Glory repeats,
His undifmay'd Legions, invincible Fleets;
Whom nor Caftles or Rocks can from Honour retard,
Since e'en Death for their King, they with Scorn difregard.

III.

O, but fee a Cloud burfts, and an Angel appears;
'Tis peace, lovely Virgin, difhevell'd!——in Tears!
Say, Fame, cry'd the Maid, is't not Time to give o'er,
With Sieges, and Famine, Explofions, and Gore?

IV.

IV.

His juſt Right to aſſert, hath the King amply try'd,
Nor his Wiſdom or Strength can Opponents abide;
Then no longer in Rage let dread Thunders be hurl'd,
But leave him to me, and give Eaſe to the World.

V.

'Tis done,——and great *George* is to Mercy inclin'd ;
The bleſt Word is gone forth for the Good of Mankind :
'Tis the Act of a *Briton* to beat, then to ſpare ;
And our King is a *Briton* ;——deny it who dare.

VI.

Charge your Glaſſes Lip high, and drink Health to the
    King,
To the Duke and the Princeſs, and make the Air ring;
May the Days of great *George* be all happy and long,
And the * Man ſtill be right, who yet never was wrong.

* Mr. Secretary *Pitt.*

The G I P S E Y.

I.

NOW the Meads are all clad with fresh Verdure
   again,
  And the Hawthorns are powder'd with White,
And Cowslips and Daizies enamel the Plain,
  And the Notes of the Cuckoo delight.
Come small ones and great ones, ye low and ye high,
And cross a young Gipsey who ne'er told a Lie.

II.

Be assur'd that our King will be blest all his Days,
 In his Consort and Progeny fair;
That Commerce shall flourish, and Glory shall blaze,
 And *Great Britain* be Heaven's chief Care.
And of this I am certain, 'tis all in my Eye,
Believe a young Gipsey who ne'er told a Lie.

III.

III.

Whilft the great ones at Helm keep their Matters all right,
  Why your Soldiers and Sailors muft beat :
Let a Chief they love head 'em, I warrant they fight,
  Both the Lads of the Camp and the Fleet.
        And of this I am certain, &c.
        Believe a young Gipfey, &c.

IV.

For the Law and the Gown, true Refpect we owe both;
  And the Faults are their own if unpaid ;
But tho' never fo queer fome will fwallow the Oath,
  And fome make a Jeft of their Trade.————
        And of this I am certain, &c.
        Believe a young Gipfey, &c.

V.

If Mechanics who fot at the Alehoufe all Day,
  And rail at they cannot tell what,
Wou'd think more of their Labour, and lefs of their Play,
  They'd be happier, I promife them that.————
        And of this I am certain, &c.
        Believe a young Gipfey, &c.

VI.

Ye fair Maids of the Ifle, of all States and Degrees,
  Think the Seafon as fatal as gay ;————
Beware whom you fip with, your Wines, and your Teas,
  And remember that Men will betray.————
        And of this I am certain, &c.
        Believe a young Gipfey, &c.

A

A New SONG.

I.

 N the reaching a Goldfinch's Neft,
  Lyfetta, the young and the fair,
  A Thorn hap't to run in her Breaft,
   Her Neighbour—the Shepherd was there.

II.

Pale and trembling he flew to her Aid ;
  She fweetly her Eyes on him fix'd ;————
His Hand on the Wound he foft laid,
  Where Rofes and Snow-drops were mix'd.

III.

But how fatal that Pity might prove,
  He knew not ; for, ah, he'd no Art ;
Till fnapt by the crocodile Love,
  His Tendernefs coft him his Heart.————

O

IV.

IV.

E're the Village Cock wakens the Morn,
  The Woodlands he pines thro' alone ;
To free the Maid's Breast from the Thorn,
  Far deeper he wounded his own.

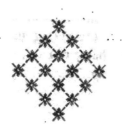

An Occasional P R O L O G U E,

Wrote at the Requeft of the Mafter of a capital
Boarding School near *London*, for one of the
young Gentlemen to fpeak before the Reprefen-
tation of the *Recruiting Officer*, at which were
prefent a numerous and elegant Auditory, 1762.

M A Y Health, Wealth, Pleafure, join exhauftlefs
       Stores,
    To gild, O blooming Fair, your circling Hours !
      And may ye never tafte one Heart felt Care,
To rob your Cheeks of thofe fweet Smiles they wear.
By thofe, our throbbing Fears are chas'd away ;
And thus embolden'd we fubmit our Play ;
Rememb'ring ftill, that every Merit fhewn,
Is to our Tutor due ;————each Fault, our own.
Moft welcome all, to this our friendly Treat:
Expect not, Gentles, here, high relifh'd Meat,
Dainty Exotics brought from *Rome* or *France*,
The warbling Signior, or the unmeaning Dance ;
Or that we call to Aid our well-wrought Scenes,
Gay tinfell'd Robes, or patch'd Coat Harlequins :
To feaft your Minds,————there centers all our Cares ;
All elfe the Tafk of mercenary Players,

For

For Bread oblig'd to break thro' Reafon's Rules,
And pleafe with Puppet-Shews an Age of Fools;
Who, fcarcely warm'd by *Shakefpear*'s hallow'd Fire, ⎫
At *Tiddidol*'s and *Jonathan*'s admire; ⎬
Burft at the Wicker Egg,— and dote upon the Wire. ⎭
To fuch dull Stuff we here wave all Pretence,
And decorate with Nature, Wit, and Senfe;
In thefe our Bard excell'd; and from his Plays,
On this we fix'd, as fitteft for thefe Days.
Since now, as when 'twas wrote, our Arms advance,
Again to curb the daftard Slaves of *France*.
Ne'er cou'd we boaft more gallant Deeds than now;
Laurels on Laurels fee entwine the Brow
Of your lov'd Monarch, *Britons*, *George* the Third:
Oh, on my Friends, by Emulation ftirr'd,
Join to recruit him; Men and Money bring,
And bravely rifque your all, to ferve your King.

C O N T E N T,

Where moſt likely to be found.

I.

 T is not Youth can give Content,
Nor is it Wealth can fee ;
It is a Dower from Heaven ſent,
But not to thee, or me.——

II.

It is not in the Monarch's Crown,
Who wou'd give Millions for't ;
It dwells not with his Grace's Frown,
Or waits on him to Court.——

III.

It is not in a Coach and Six,
It is not in a Garter ;
'Tis not in Love or Politics,
But 'tis in——*Will* the Carter:

T

The COMPLAINT.

A SONG.

I.

WHEN *Phillis* first, in homespun Gray,
  Her Lambkins white cou'd feed,
With us cou'd innocently play,
  Or dance, or sing, or read.———

II.

I priz'd her far above the Earth,
  Nor wou'd have ever chang'd;
But soon she scorn'd my humble Birth,
  And from the Cottage rang'd.———

III.

My Crook and Flock she once did love,
  Nay vow'd for them she'd scorn
Vain Pomp or Shew, nor quit the Grove;
  But *Phillis* is forsworn.

IV.

IV.

Tempted by Gugaws, Balls and Plays,
  She flies lefs guilty Scenes;
Contemns my Pipe for *Stanley*'s Lays,
  For Routes, our Wakes and Greens.————

V.

Our Sports by Moon-light fhe forfakes,
  For Flambeaux, Crowd and Noife;
Barters, for flimfy worthlefs Rakes,
  The Sweet that never cloys.

VI.

Yet ,*Phyllis*, tho' you revel now,
  Too foon, fond Maid, you'll find
The Difference 'twixt that thing a Beau,
  And *Strephon*'s fteadier Mind.

A SONG.

Set by Mr. *C. Festing,* and sung by Mrs. *Storer,* at
Ranelaigh.

I.

WELCOME Sun! 'and southern Showers!
Harbingers of Buds and Flowers,
Welcome Grots, and cooling Shades!
Farewel Balls, and Masquerades!———

II.

Blooming *May* approacheth near,
The Lowing of the Herds we hear;
The fat'ning Lambs around us bleat,
Whilst Daizies spring beneath their Feet.

III.

Perch'd are the Birds on every Spray,
Stretching their Throats to praise the Day;
A thousand Herbs their Fragrance yield,
And Cowslips cover all the Field.

IV.

IV.

Sure 'tis more than Time we flee,
London, from thy Smoke and thee ;
Welcome Joys, more pure and true ;
Drums and Routes, adieu ! adieu !

On

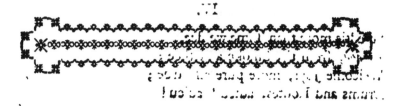

On the Marriage of the Right Honourable the Earl of Kildare with Lady Caroline Lenox, Daughter of his Grace the Duke of Richmond.

NATURE hath long been ranſack'd of her Store,
For *Phyllis, Chloe,* and ten thouſand more;
Roſe,--Lilly,--Pink,--been ſtript from native Bed,
To deck the Wench of each fantaſtic Head.
But now they droop; their envious Colours gone;
Lenox appears! with Beauties all her own.———
Her charming Face———incomparable Maid,—
Diſdains to ſeek their unavailing Aid.
So noble,—virtuous,—witty, and ſo fair,
So good, ſo perfect are the happy Pair;
Rancour ſtands mute, when Fame preſents *Kildare.*

N O

III.

PATTY JENKYNS.

A SONG.

Tune, *Daniel Cooper.*

I.

WHO d'ye think I met laft Night,
    In all her Airs, and Prinkings,
    With Tippet rough, and Velvet Muff,
      But blowzy *Patty Jenkyns?*
Tho' now a Belle, I know her well,
    When Butter-milk fhe carried ;
Her Father cry'd round Tan to fell ;
    Ned Flaharty fhe married.

II.

Ned ran to Sea, and then with me,
    Or any one that catch'd her,
For Chink and Fame fhe'd play a Game,
    At which few over-match'd her.
Prefuming on the ancient Scheme,
    And being fomewhat fifkey,—
I took a Whim to ftop the Brim,
    And booze a Cogue of Whifkey.

III.

III.

Get out, you dirty Dog, said she,
  Such Pimps I give the Bag now;
With gallant Pride in Chair I ride,
  And Sattin wear, and Shag too.
In Box I sit, and twig the Pit:
  My Keeper's Colonel *Rake*, Sir;
And if with me you dare make free,
  His Man shall crack your Chake, Sir.

IV.

Said I, my Dear, be not severe,
  Good Faith, I meant to plaise you;
But since so high you throw your Eye,
  Why *Bryant*'s Heart is aify.——
Sure I'm as free as you, d'y'see,
  I'll morris to my Drinkings;
As Money's scarce,——there a Kick o'the A——
  And your Servant, Madam *Jenkyns*.

HIBERNIA.

An ODE.

In Compliment to the original Promoters of, and
Contributors to the Premiums given annually for
the Encouragement of Trades, Arts and Sciences,
as it was to have been performed at the Music-Hall
in *Fishamble-street*, for the Benefit of the poor
Lunatics in the Hospital founded by the late Dean
Swift.—The Music compos'd by Mr. *Broadway*,
Organist of *Christ-Church* and *St. Ann's, Dublin*.

RECITATIVE.

O H blooming Circle!—O enchanting Fair!
  Whose beauteous Bosoms heave at Pity's Call,
  What Praise can paint enough, your gentle Care
  Of real Objects,—helpless and forlorn ?—

AIR.

Destin'd for ever to remain,
  By keenest Woes opprest ;
Till Death dissolves the cruel Chain,
  And gives eternal Rest.

RECIT.

RECIT.

The baneful Clouds of Indolence diffolv'd,
Induftry rears her modeft awful Head;
And thus fhe chaunts;——but firft, from brimming Lid,
The Pearl parental wipes—the exulting Tear.

AIR.

I joy to behold the new Edifice rife,
The Helplefs to fuccour, to foften their Cries;
In Times yet to come, may the innocent Race,
Upheld by Compaffion, your Tendernefs grace.
    Soldiers, to enhance your Glory;
    Clerks profound, to pen your Story;
    Tradefmen, to enrich the Nation;—
    O how worthy Prefervation!——

RECIT.

Encouragement,—the great Support of Trade,
Of fcientific Skill, and liberal Arts,
With undiffembled Joy we mean to fing,
Accept a Tribute to your Bounty's due.

GRAND CHORUS.

O may glorious Rays divine,
Round each Brow eternal fhine;
Who by Premiums given for Toil,
Firft rais'd our late dejected Ifle.

RECIT.

RECIT.

Where lofty Veſſels once ſecurely rode,
Whilſt bounding Billows brav'd the azure Sky,
The Peaſant ſtalks, elate with jocund Glee,
To view the Fruits of his aſſiduous Care,
The golden, waving, gay, luxuriant Field.——

AIR.

Old *Dermot* planted on the Plain
What *Ted* enjoys;—a jolly Swain,
   Rich Cyder tops the Bowl:
To *Shelah* ſeated on his Knees,
He boaſts his Lands, his Herds, his Trees,
   And opens all his Soul.

GRAND CHORUS.

O may glorious Rays, &c.

RECIT.

The wide, extenſive, dry, and barren Waſte,
The rocky Clift, the dreary pathleſs Dale,
O bleſt Tranſition! we at length behold,
Grac'd with the Charms of Plenty's beauteous Train.

AIR.

The gladſome Eye with Wonder ſees,
New Groves around of thick'ning Trees;
The Meadows rich with bleating Sheep,
While wanton Kids the Summits ſkip,

All along the flowery Glen,
Sport the Nymphs, and happy Men!
Who'd not wish a Life like this,
To fold the Flock, and then to kifs?

CHORUS.

O may glorious Rays, &c.

RECIT:

Ye truly wife! whofe hofpitable Cares,
Thro' Labour's Road point out the Path to Blifs.
Your rich, your vaft Increafe, each annual Round
Shall ftrike, and emulate the neighbouring States.

AIR.

Mechanics of this happy Ifle,
    Juft Heaven implore with grateful Hearts!—
To blefs thofe Hands that crown your Toil;
    The great Rewarders of your Arts.
Firm Patriots who their Country prize,
    Beyond extremeft earthly Boon,
Who Wealth import from diftant Skies,
    And teach ye to improve your own.

RECIT,

Proud, avaritious, unrelenting Souls,
Who never knew what foft Compaffion meant,
Find no Employment here; but ftand aloof,
And fwell with Envy, at your Virtue's Tale.

AIR.

AIR.

Sound, found thy Trump, immortal Fame ! ——
Hibernia through the World proclaim ;
   All friendly, good and kind ;
Who Balm applies to each Difeafe,
And whilft the fhackl'd Corpfe fhe frees,
   She captivates the Mind.

P   From

From a SAILOR on board the *Bridgwater* Man of War, Lord *George Graham* Commander, to a former Mess-mate at *Chatham*, on their finking, and driving on Shore seven of the Enemies Ships, with three only in Company, in the Year 1744.

A S O N G.

Tune, *Abbot of* Canterbury.

I.

THE News you may credit, dear *Jack*, that I send,
'Tis of an Engagement we've had at *Ostend*;
Where, glorious Recital!—the Truth I advance,
Three Ships of *Old England* beat seven of *France*.
  Derry down, &c.

II.

With haughty Bravados, boast *Gallia* no more;
We have thumpt you at Sea, and we'll thump you on
    Shore,
You'll never find *Britain* in haste to agree,
Whilst *William*'s in *Flanders*, or *Graham* at Sea.
  Derry down, &c.

III.

III.

At *Tournay* ye beat us; 'twill do ye no good,
For each Spoonful we loft, we'll have Gallons of Blood:
Till the *English* are hurt they are always too civil;
But fting 'em once home, and they'll fight like the D——l.

　　　　　　　　　　Derry down, &c.

IV.

Your Puffs are all Wind, and no Merit enhance;
Tho' ye open'd the Ball, yet we'll have the laft Dance.
Ye've hoifted your Flag, but we'll make ye foon ftrike it;
Or play fuch a Jig, 'tis a Chance if you like it.

　　　　　　　　　　Derry down, &c.

V.

Thus the *Bridgwater* fpoke, and went to it pell-mell;
And *Gordon* and *Fergufon* fought too like H——l;
Arms and Legs flew about like a Shower of Hail,
And what Heads were left on——thought it beft to turn
　　　　Tail.

　　　　　　　　　　Derry down, &c.

VI.

Moft Chriftian-like King! had your Majefty feen
An Action like this, 'twou'd have fill'd you with Spleen;
From our Scoopers ran Blood of your Subjects fo rare,
Who are now cutting Caprioles Heaven knows where.

　　　　　　　　　　Derry down, &c.

VII.

VII.

With the Old *British* Spirit we drove three afhore ;
Took and funk all the reft ; and what cou'd we do more?.
At Sight of this,—drink to Lord *Graham* all good,
And wifh their whole Navy as faft in the Mud. .

      Derry down, &c.

Nature

Nature *againſt* G------k, *for ſtealing her Beauties.*

WHAT! ſhall Ingratitude, deteſted Weed!—
On thy fair Stem, my favorite Bloſſom feed?—
Was it for this I faſhion'd thee with Care,
    Gave thee a Tinct of every thing that's rare;
Taught thee to ſmooth the harraſs'd Stateſman's Frown,
T'amaze the Bar, the Senate, and the Gown;
T'inſtruct and model a licentious Town,
The Cit, the Wit, the Coxcomb, and the Clown.———
Review'd with Caution every human Breaſt,
And where I found ſuperior Worth poſſeſs'd,
That Worth I cull'd;——I robb'd it of its due,
To make an eſtimable Boon for you.
Envy and Malice ſtand aghaſt to ſee
What Heaps of Favours I've beſtow'd on thee;
Have I deny'd you any thing you ſu'd?——
Why then this Treatment barbarouſly rude?
Why purloin Helps you might be ſure I'd give:
Why to delude thy tender Parent ſtrive?——
Wretch as thou art!——

P 3   I came

I came to chide thee, *David*; but how wild
Are Mother's Threats, when doting on the Child!
Perhaps, in lieu of Anger, thou might'ft fee
New Favours flowing;—cou'd they flow from me!
But thou haft quite exhaufted all my Store;
And Nature wants the Power of giving more,

THE
F R O L I C K S *of* M A Y.

An Interlude of Singing and Dancing.

The Music by Mr. Patterfal.

Scene, an open pleasant Country. Numbers of Shepherds and Shepherdesses appear at some Distance, preparing to dance round their May-pole.

Enter Spring hastily — Winter, following feebly, and in a supplicating Manner, sings.

AIR.

AY, dear Partner, Spring, be not angry, I pray,
That once in this Island I've made such a Stay:
But the Wood-Nymphs so trim, the Shepherds so gay,
I long'd for a Peep at the Frolicks of *May*.

Spring

Spring sings.

Dotard ! with that furrow'd Face,
Stranger to all Joy and Grace :
Humid Eyes and tottering Pace,
Ill befit this charming Place.
Where Thunders roll, and Lightnings glance,
On blasted Heaths where Devils dance,
With *Lapland* Hags, and Priests from *France*,
Thou shou'd'st have been this many a Day :
Hie, hie thee hence !—be gone—away,
For see the sweet, the blooming *May*.

Exit Winter.

Enter May.

O welcome, welcome, lovely *May*.

May sings.

Kind Spring, thy warm Friendship, with Rapture I see,
Hath once again fill'd this rich Island with Glee :
The Mounts are all rob'd with their Mantles of Green;
My Hawthorns are white, as they ever were seen :
Soft Bleatings are heard from Hill, Valley, and Plain,
And the Groves all re-eccho with Warblers again.

Enter Flora, and sings.

Tribute, gentle Spring, I pay
To thee, and to thy Sister *May*,
Of the Cowslip and the Rose,
And every Child that Nature grows :
On ev'ry Brow, in ev'ry Glen,
Thro' ev'ry Mead, or Bog, or Fen :
Mine shall be to deck the Ground
With dainty Garb. 'gainst you come round.

Spring

Spring sings.

Guardians of the sylvan Plains,
Smirking Nymphs and jolly Swains,
Labour not this live-long Day,
Hither come—with Speed away,
To sing, and to drink, and to dance, and to play,
And to join all alike in the Frolicks of *May*.

All join in the grand Dance, which concludes the Scene.

A HUNTING SONG.

RECITATIVE.

NOW peeps the ruddy Dawn o'er Mountain Top,
 Its different Notes each feather'd Warbler tunes,
 The Milkmaid's Carrol glads the Ploughman's
            Ear,
The jolly Huntſman winds his chearful Horn,
And the ſtaunch Pack return the lov'd Salute.

AIR.

The Hounds are unkennel'd, and now,
   Thro' the Copſe and the Furze will we lead,
Till we reach yonder Farm on the Brow,
   For there lurks the Thief that muſt bleed.
I told you ſo, didn't I?—ſee where he flies:
'Twas *Bellman* that open'd, ſo ſure the Fox dies.
     Let the Horn's jolly Sound
     Encourage the Hound,
And float thro' the ecchoing Skies.

RECITATIVE.

The Chace began, nor Rock, nor Flood, nor Swamp,
Quickſet, or Gate, the thundering Courſe retard;
Till the dead Notes proclaim the fallen Prey,
Then—to the ſportive 'Squire's capacious Bowl.

AIR.

AIR.

O'er that and old Beer of his own,
That is found, bright, and wholfome we'll fing,
Drink Succefs to great *George* and his Crown,
For each Heart to a Man's with the King.
And next will we fill to *Jove's* favorite Scene,
The rich Ifle of *Britain, Great-Britain* I mean;
Where Men, Horfes and Hounds,
Can be ftopt by no Bounds,
For no Spot on the Earth e'er bred Sporters fo keen,

A

A BACCHANALIAN SONG.

STRANGER to the pensive Brow,
  To the Bosom damp'd with Care,
To the languid love-sick Vow,
  All the Plagues that great ones share;
Waiter, bring me t'other Flask,
'Twill make but six, a slender Task.

II.

Bane to me the plaintive Sigh,
  I doat on jolly Cheek and red,
Hence, far hence, the woe worn Eye,
  And come, brisk Laughter, in its Stead.
Away and crown our Flasks and Bowls,
For Night's the Holiday of Souls.

III.

Jove may give to whom he will,
  Treasures of the golden Mine;
Devotee to *Bacchus* still,
  I'll never seek another shrine;
But sing and dance and kiss and quaff,
And make the World a World of Laugh.

A

A S O N G.

I.

FOR me, O Tyrant, Love, thy Snare,
 And all thy Baits delufive ceafe ;
Thou art the Fountain-head of Care,
 The Murderer of Sleep and Peace.

II.

A fell Hyena to the Heart,
 That lulls us on but to deftroy ;
An ill-far'd Canker-worm thou art,
 That blights our Years of Eafe and Joy.

III.

To me, O Goddefs fage, thine Ear
 To me, *Minerva*, deign to lend ;
What Ills betide me, let me ne'er
 To cruel *Cupid*'s Power bend.

IV.

IV.

My Suit is granted, and I now
    Am light as Air, am gay and free;
Blind Boy, I scorn thy fatal Bow,
    I laugh at *Damon*'s Arts and thee.

For.

The EASTER-HOLIDAYS:

A SONG.

As now fung by Mr. *Andrews*, at *Sadler's Wells*.

I.

ITHER, hither, young and gay,
Hither, hither, hafte away ;
Now's the Time to fport and play,
When all the World keep Holiday.
Holiday, Holiday,
When all the World keep Holiday.

II.

Now the Laffes, mild as *May*,
Will not, cannot anfwer Nay,
They mind not what the old ones fay,
For all the world keep Holiday.
Holiday, Holiday,
For all the World keep Holiday.

III.

III.

Blackbirds whiftle from the Spray,
Merry, merry founds the Lay
Of Swain, who lets the Lambkins ftray,
While all the World keep Holiday.
Holiday, Holiday,
While all the World keep Holiday.

IV.

Shepherd, welcome do we pay,
Strike up rural Roundelay,
Whisk it, frisk it, Girls away,
For all the World keep Holiday.
Holiday, Holiday,
For all the World keep Holiday.

On

On her *Majesty, Queen* CHARLOTTE's
Arrival in England.

A SONG.

RECITATIVE.

WHEN *Neptune* late to royal *George* convey'd
Thro' briny Surge the princely blooming Maid,
On Sight of *Albion*, with pacific Stroke,
The fwelling Waves he calm'd, and thus he
fpoke.

I.

To *Great Bretain*, Ifle of mine,
Gladly bring I Boon divine,
Send forth your cluftring Bands to greet
TheFair that makes their Blifs compleat.

II.

Where's the Nation elfe can boaft
Of a Freedom ne'er yet loft?
Of fuch a Monarch, young and great,
So priz'd by Subjects and by Fate?

Q

III.

III.

Where can Statesmen such be found?
Soldiers, Sailors, brave and sound?
Where else doth Science rear its Head?
Or where can Art so well be fed?

IV.

In what Forests say where grows
Oaks like *Britain's*? Dread of Foes:
Of Flocks such Numbers where else shorn?
Or where such golden Fields of Corn?

V.

Yet a Wanting still was here;
George your Monarch heav'd with Care;
A Wife of peerless Worth he sought,
And see young *Charlotte* safe I brought.

JOHNNY

JOHNNY *and* BETSY,

Sung this Seafon at *Sadler's Wells.*

I.

MY Daddy was gone to the Market a Mile,
My Mammy was gone to the Miller's the while,
In came my dear *Johnny*, and fuch was his
   Saying,
Lay by your Wheel, *Betfy*, come with me a Maying.

II.

I anfwer'd him no, 'twas a Folly to ask,
My Mammy had fet me to fpinning a Task:
Quoth he cut the Tether, Girl, fet the Cow ftraying
We'll tye her up fomewhere, whilft we go a Maying.

III.

His Method I took,—ah how cou'd I forbear?
I lov'd him too well to think falfly he'd fwear;
He prefs'd my Lips gently, the Fool fell to playing,
The Time flipt fo nimbly, we didn't go Maying.

IV.

My Daddy ne'er afk'd me a Word where I'd been,
My Mammy I told I'd the Cow to fetch in,
She faid fhe was fure I'd been fomewhere delaying,
But never fufpected that I'd been a Maying.

V.

V.

If *Johnny* prove's true, as I think that he will,
The Market I'll blefs, and I'll honour the Mill,
That kept my old Daddy and Mammy fo ftaying,
When I was perfuaded by *Johnny* a Maying.

A Loyal S O N G,

Sung this Seafon at *Sadler's Wells.*

I.

'TIS the Genius of *Britain,* ye *Britons,* that calls;
Quit your Glaffes and Laffes for Powder and Balls;
To the lovefick Guittar be the Trumpet preferr'd;
And threfh well the Foes of your King, *George* the Third:
 The Work was well done,
 And made excellent Fun,
In Seventeen Hundred and Sixty-one.
 Be as gallant and true,
 And I warrant you'll do,
In Seventeen Hundred and Sixty-two.

II.

'Tis the Thundring of Cannon, the Rattle of Drums;
The Deftruction of Cities, the routing of Scums;
'Tis your Freedom to fave, and your Rights, now at ftake;
That all fummon ye hence a due Vengeance to take:
 The Work was well done,
 And made excellent Fun,
In Seventeen Hundred and Sixty-one:
 Be as gallant and true,
 And I warrant you'll do,
In Seventeen Hundred and Sixty-two.

III.

III.

See the Marquis, how bold and how noble he ftands!
For his Orders how quiet, how ready the Bands!
See his flafhing Steel drawn, and hark how the Air rings!
With Shouts of Revenge 'gainft the league-breaking Kings!
  The Work was well done,
  And made excellent Fun,
 In Seventeen Hundred and Sixty-one;
  Be as gallant and true,
  And I warrant 'twill do
In Seventeen Hundred and Sixty-two.

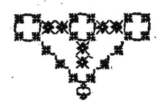

On

ON THE
ORATORIO *of* JOSHUA.

I.

O N *Wednesday* laſt *Jupiter* taking his Rounds,
And with Care reconnoitring his heavenly
Bounds,
A Harmony ſweeter than that of the Spheres,
Aſcended from Earth to the Thunderer's Ears.

II.

I cannot imagine, ſaid he, why *Apollo*,
This ſneaking, this pitiful Cuſtom will follow ;
His Muſic, his Wit, and his Company's given
To the Clods o' the Earth, whilſt we want it in Heaven.

III.

Old *Momus*, the Joker, a Pardon deſir'd,
Then told him the Sounds which he heard and admir'd
Came not from *Apollo* he very well knew,
And if he'd ſtep down, he'd convince him 'twas true.

Q 4　　　　　　　　　　IV.

IV.

Jove seldom was out at a Frolic as yet,
And flap they appear'd in the Midft of the Pit;
But when of bright Beauties he faw fuch a Throng,
He wonder'd that *Britain* had 'fcap'd him fo long.

V.

In the Form of an Orange he thought he might venture
To the Lips of my Lady, who fat in the Centre;
But found 'em fo chafte, that, repenting his folly,
His Shape he refum'd. and attended to *Galli.*

VI.

Enraptur'd he figh'd, then to *Mercury* faid,
Calliope's nothing, compar'd with this Maid;
Or fweet *Caffarini*, whofe warbling Strains
Might furely footh *Sifyphus* out of his Pains.

VII.

And prithee what's *Orpheus*, when mention'd with *Lowe?*
'Tis true at his Voice and the Touch of his Bow
He made Pebbles dance; but *Lowe*'s filver Tone
The *Thracian* himfelf wou'd have chang'd to a Stone.

VIII.

For *Handel*, his Mufic fo highly I prize,
I'll fend *Phœbus* here, and take him to the Skies;
The Difference Men may not eafily find,
Since Gods to fuch Merit fo long have been blind.

E P I-

E P I L O G U E,

Spoke by Mafter ——, who play'd the Part of
Silvia in the *Recruiting Officer*, at —— Boarding-
School, the Night before breaking up for the
Holidays.

I Make no doubt ye have felt, fo need not ask,
The Joy refulting from the finifh'd Task ;
At mine, of courfe, well qualified to guefs,
You can't but think I tafte it to Excefs :
How my poor Heart hath all this Ev'ning beat !——
Tho' confcious of the Candor we fhou'd meet.
As Actor firft full many a Scruple rofe ;
Then to appear drawn forth in Womens Cloaths :
Such unmatch'd Sweetnefs dwells in Female Features,
That when we ape them, fure we are horrid Creatures.
But to Neceffity the wifeft bend,
And wink on the Omiffions of a Friend.
Right noble Spirits ne'er in queftion call
The Gift, tho' poor, that is the Giver's All.
On thefe trite Maxims here we reft our Caufe :
What fays our Counfel, learned in the Laws ? ——
Stand we acquitted of all wilful Errors?
Be hufh'd, my Heart, I fee no Brow of Terrors.
We'll think we've pleas'd ye then ; yet let me fay,
We'll pleafe you better ftill another Day.

By

By conſtant Practice 'tis Men maſter Arts;
So, mellow grown, and eaſier in our Parts,
Theſe Scenes at our Return we ſhall repeat;
The ſelf-ſame Audience hope again to meet:
Faults of this Night we'll ſtudy to retrieve;
For Favours paſt our general Thanks receive:
Ladies and Gentlemen, we take our leave.

A BALLAD.

Vrote foon after the Declaration of War againſt
Spain.

Sung this Seaſon at *Sadler's Wells.*

I.

OUND out on a Cruiſe, no Tar wou'd refuſe,
    I've ſtow'd in compleatly my Store ;
Two Hundred bold Men I command once again,
    And ſhall ſhortly fall down to the *Nore.*
ve Room for a Score or two, enter, Boys, quick ;
Pound to a Shilling we make the Dogs ſick.

II.

Days of Queen *Beſs*—we now are no leſs,
    Spain's vaunting Armado we beat ;
nd at it poor *France* fell into a Trance,
    That ſhe hasn't recover'd of yet ;
Puffs only Rich, of her Treaſure ſhe's rid,
Ve'll deal the ſame Cards to the Dons at *Madrid.*

III.

III.

Midſt Fire and Smoke, when we give 'em a Stroke,
    The tawney Bravadoes ſhall fly;
Nor Prieſt, Bell, or Book, ſhall ſecure 'em good Luck;
    As ſure as they face us they die.
Saints, Wafers and Rags ſhall be blown into Air,
When once we have brought but our great Guns to bear.

IV.

Safe anchor'd, my Boys, in Port of our Joys,
    Snug under the Guard of our Guns,
Their Convents we'll ſtrip, and freight home the rich Ship
    With the Plunder of Prieſts and of Nuns.
Then ſpeed *The New Terrible* well, and Hurra!
And ſend her ſafe into the the proud *Panama*.

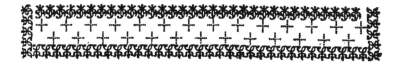

A BACCHANALIAN SONG.

Sung by Mrs. *Atkins* at *Sadler's Wells*.

I.

COME booze, my Lads, booze ; puſh the Bottle
    about,
  Ye Ninnies, for whom wou'd you ſave ?
Your Wife, with her Fondneſs who makes ſuch
    a Rout,
  She'll laugh 'ere you're cold in your Grave.
Mankind are mere Shams wear what Vizors they pleaſe
The only true Friends are fair Bumpers and Eaſe.

II.

Do you ſcrape for a Son, whom with Coſt and with Care
  You have hitherto anxiouſly bred ?
The firſt in the Chamber ſhall be the young Heir,
  To Pluck Pillow from under your Head.
Nunc, nunc eſt bibendum, our Motto you ſee,
Stick, ſtick to it cloſe, and be happy as we.

III.

III.

For Friend, or for Miſtreſs ar't heaping thy Store?
  Ah Trifler!—but little you know!
An Ear-ring perverts your bright Saint to a W——e;
  Diſtreſs of your Friend makes a Foe.
What need of Advice againſt hoarding of Pelf?
A Bumper, a Bumper will ſpeak for itſelf.

IV.

Haſte, haſte ye to us, and but do as we do,
  I warrant you ne'er will repent:
The Tale of a Tub is both merry and true,
  I ne'er knew what other Tales meant.
Let 'em preach, let 'em fight, let 'em cavil and brawl,
A Bumper and Eaſe I prefer to 'em all.

THE

THE

HEIRESS.

THE

HEIRESS;

OR,

ANTIGALLICAN.

A

FARCE.

R

Dramatis Personæ.

M E N.

BRriton, fen. a Country Gentleman,   *Mr.* Burton.
    Briton, jun. (his Son) bred in Town,   *Mr.* Packer.
Dafh, a Coxcomb,   *Mr.* Palmer.
Capt. *Hardy,* a Sea Officer,   *Mr.* Yates.
Wortby, his Purfer,   *Mr.* Beard.
French Valet,   *Mr.* Weft.
Englifh Servant to *Briton,* jun.   *Mr.* Grey.
Englifh Servant to Lady *Everbloom.*   *Mr.* Watkins.

W O M E N.

Lady *Everbloom,* Sifter to Capt. *Hardy,*   *Mrs.* Simpfon.
Mrs. *Spruce,* a Milliner,   *Mrs.* Bradfhaw.
Harriot (the Heirefs) difguis'd as a Boy
    on a Family Affair, in Love with *Bri-* } *Mifs* Barton.
    ton, jun.
Letitia, Daughter to Mr. *Briton,* in Love
    with *Harriot,* being ignorant of her } *Mifs* Hipfley.
    Sex,
Mifs *Dolly* }
    and } Apprentices to Mrs. *Spruce,* { *Mifs* Bride,
Mifs *Pen,* } and { *Mifs* Simpfon.
Mifs *Belmont,* } { *Mifs* Arabella Young.
Mifs *Languifh,* } Vifiting Ladies, { *Mrs.* Smith.
Mifs *Giddy,* &c. } { *Mifs* Mills.

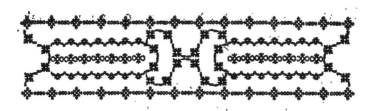

THE

HEIRESS.

ACT I.

SCENE, *A Parlour.*

Enter Mr. Briton, *fen. with his Hat, Gloves, Cane and Sword, as juft come in* ; *Mrs.* Spruce *following him.*

Briton, fen.

AND where are our young Folks, pray Madam?

Mrs. *Spruce.*

Abroad, Sir; I think I heard 'em mention the Park.

Briton,

Briton, fen.

It's very fine Weather, and they are quite right to take the Benefit of it.

Mrs. *Spruce.*

I hope, Sir, you have met with things anfwerable to your Expectations, at leaft————

Briton, fen.

I thank you, Madam, I have ;————I believe I fhall now, very fhortly, fee an End to my Affair; the Earl is moft certainly a worthy Nobleman, when once you can get at him ; but there is fuch a Gulph of Ignorance, Impertinence and Adulation to wade through, before one can be admitted to the Ears of the Great, as makes it very fatiguing to a plain Man like myfelf, to have any Sort of Bufinefs to tranfact with them.

Mrs. *Spruce.*

Undoubtedly right, Sir ; but thofe who have Occafion to follicit their Favours, muft put up with fuch Inconveniencies.

Briton, fen.

I thank Heaven, my Eftate, though fmall, is entirely free from Dependence ; but to ferve an Orphan intrufted to one's Care, is a Duty fo incumbent on a Man of Principle, that he would undertake any reafonable Tafk (however unpleafant) rather than leave fuch Bufinefs unfettled.

Mrs. *Spruce.*

Certainly, Sir.

Briton, fen.

That once done, I don't care how foon I turn my Back upon *London*: I want my ufual Study and Exercife; a Town Life is a miferable one to me.

Enter Briton, *junior.*

Oh, *Bob!* where have you left your Companions?

Briton, jun.

At the next Door, Sir, buying fome Toys.

Enter Mifs Pen.

You are wanted in the Shop, Madam. [*To Mrs.* Spruce.

Mrs. Spruce.

Gentlemen, your Servant. [*Exit Mrs.* Spruce.

Briton, fen.

Madam, your moft obedient———Well, and where have you been, *Bob*, ha?

Briton, jun.

In *Hydepark*, Sir; there was Abundance of Company: Coming back we call'd in at *Cack*'s, and look'd at the Machine that goes without Horfes: there were feveral People of Quality there; and I affure you, our young Gentleman made no infignificant Figure among 'em from the

R 3 Que-

Queſtions that he aſk'd Mr. *Ladd* the Proprietor, in regard to his new invented Mechaniſm.

Briton, ſen.

O! he has been bred with great Care; and, though never before from Home, has had the beſt Tuition the Country afforded.

Briton, jun.

He ſeems very fond of my Siſter *Letty,* I think.

Briton, ſen.

Ay: [*ſighing*] it is ſome time ſince that I have obſerv'd it, not without Compunction; and have uſed all the Means in my Power to damp, in the Kindling, a Flame that may one Day prove fatal in its Conſequences; but the Nearneſs of our Neighbourhood, with the great Intimacy between Sir *Aſton* and myſelf, hath hitherto render'd it impracticable.

Briton, jun.

Did you never drop a Hint, Sir, of any Surmiſe you had concerning the growing Paſſion between 'em?

Briton, ſen.

O! yes! often: but whenever I did, the Knight uſed to turn it off with ſome pleaſant Conceit, as a Subject not worth Notice: I had ſome Thoughts once of removing to a more diſtant Part of the Country; but he inſiſted on my ſtaying where I was. The Buſineſs that call'd me to *London,* furniſh'd me with a good Pretence to bring the the Girl off, by way of ſatisfying her Curioſity, and leaving her behind me; but Sir *Aſton* inſiſted ſo ſtrongly upon

his

his Son's keeping us Company, that there was no deny
ing him ; and————

Briton, jun.

Suppose, Sir, as you design writing to *Newgrove* this
Afternoon, you were to touch upon the Matter a little
stronger than you have hitherto done ; and hear what he'll
say upon it.

Briton, sen.

I did mention it in my last, to which I am surpriz'd I have
had no Answer yet ; a Repetition this Evening wou'd n't be
amiss, as you say. You cannot be insensible, *Bob*, of the wide
Disparity of Fortune between the Families ; and if any
Accident shou'd happen that might cause my Honour, or
Reputation, to be suspected, it wou'd be worse than Death
to me.

Briton, jun.

By the strictest Observation I have been able to form,
Sir, I see nothing in either of their Conducts likely to feed
such Suspicion ; but on the contrary, a regardful Deportment scarcely consistent with their times of Life.

Briton, sen.

The Manner of their Education, and the little Variety
of Company they have had the Opportunity to converse
with, accounts for that ; but————

Briton, jun.

I have sometimes wonder'd indeed, that Sir *Aston* cou'd
so readily trust an only Son and Heir, so little acquainted
with more than the Theory of Men and Things, so far
diftant

diſtant without him, and eſpecially to a Town crouded with Temptations, as this is ; but when I have conſider'd the Openneſs of his Temper, the Security repos'd in his Son's Principles, and the ſtrict Ties of a long and ſincere Friend-ſhip between you, that Wonder has ſubſided.

Briton, ſen.

His Coming was but weakly urg'd on my Side, but the young Spark had the Addreſs to make his Father believe that it was for your Sake entirely he wanted to ſee *London:* thoſe Letters of your's, he had often heard me read, had ſo much charm'd him, he pretended, that he long'd for an Opportunity of ſeeing you : on that Account a Grant was given, which, as I ſaid before, I heartily wiſh I may never hear repented.

Briton, jun.

Don't ſuffer yourſelf to be too much alarm'd, Sir; well-faſhion'd Diſpoſitions ſeldom ſubmit to Meanneſſes. I ſhall however make it my principal Concern to regard their Behaviours, and if I find the Affair we ſuſpect too forward, ſhall endeavour to turn the Tide of his Paſſion into another Channel, which, at his Age, and with a little Management, may be eaſily effected.———— O ! here they come.

Enter Harriot, *in Boys Cloaths, and* Letty.

Well, Siſter, have you and Mr. *Bellmour* adjuſted your Diſpute amicably ?

Letty.

Letty.

We never quarrel, Brother; however, I can't give up the Argument.

Briton, fen..

What was it concerning, my Dear?

Letty.

Why, Sir, Mr. *Bellmour* wou'd have it that Lady *Sparkle* is much handfomer than Mrs. *Pool,* and I can't allow it; that's all.

Briton, fen.

You know I am a Stranger to the fine Ladies of the prefent Age; and fo can fay nothing to it; both reigning Toafts, I fuppofe.

Letty.

Yes, Sir, fo I have heard; but I don't perceive much Beauty in either of them for my Part, except what they are indebted to Art for.

Harriot.

O! fye! never let Prejudice get the better of Under-ftanding; they are certainly both of 'em exceeding fine Women; I hardly know which to give the Preference—but of the two, Lady *Sparkle*—what think you, Sir?

[*To Briton,* jun.

Briton, jun.

Briton, jun.

I am of your Opinion, Mr. *Bellmour*; Lady *Sparkle* is indeed the moft agreeable. *Letty* is right, however, in her Obfervation, that they both affift Nature; but that Vice, amongft the many others for which we are indebted to *French* Luxury, is now fo univerfally practifed, that it is no longer look'd on as an Indifcretion, except by the infpired Few, ftill *English* enough to avow an Efteem for the Cuftoms and Manners of their Forefathers, and pay due Regard to Religion and Modefty.

Enter a Servant.

Mr. *Dafh*, Sir, is below.——

Briton, jun.

Defire him to walk up——   {*Exit Servant.*

Briton, fen.

I'll ftep as far as *Chancery-Lane*; you'll all dine at Home, I fuppofe.

Briton, jun.

O, yes, Sir.

Briton, fen.

Well, your Servant——   [*Exit. Briton*, fen·

Letty.

Letty.

Dash!——that's the impudent Coxcomb that pester'd
is fo abominably the other Evening in the Park; is it
not?

Briton, jun.

Yes, I wonder the Fellow didn't deny me to him; he
knows very well that I can't abide him.

Enter Dash, *finging.*

O! Mr. *Dash,* your Servant!——always gay, Sir——

Dash.

Ay, nothing like it; ever, ever fprightly——Ha!——
my *Carnifh* Buck, give me your Hand; "we'll teach you
' to drink deep e're you depart," as Friend *Shakefpear*
has it.—What, my little Modefty—A Pox o' this Country
Breeding, this Strawberry and Cream Education; you
nuft get rid on't as faft as ever you can, Child, if you expect to cut any Sort of Figure in the *Beau Monde.*
                    [*Goes up to* Letty *and kiffes her Hand.*

Letty.

If that be the only Condition of Admittance to the *Beau
Monde,* Sir, as you call it, I fhall be always defirous of
continuing a Stranger to it.

Dash.

Dash.

Ha!—ſtupid enough!—I muſt try if I can bring you into a better Notion of things, Child; for I ſhould be very ſorry to differ from one ſo pretty.

Letty.

And I am very glad to differ from one ſo pert.

Dash.

Ha, ha, ha. Upon my Word——ſomething very like a Hit, by *Venus!*——Harkee, *Briton,* 'there's ſomething clever about this Siſter of your's, I can tell you that; but ſhe wants a little of the——the——the——you under-ſtand me. Do, prithee perſuade her to ſee a little more of the World, and try her Hand at ſmall Game, before ſhe attacks Principals; for wherever I ſubdue, I give no Quarter.

Letty.

I have not the leaſt Fear of you, moſt terrible Sir; and if ever you make a Conqueſt of me, treat me juſt as you think proper; I promiſe you I'll never complain on't.

Dash.

A ſmart Wench, faith!—'tis a thouſand Pities ſhe had not been brought into Life ſooner;—but ſober Parents, country Curates, *Gothic* Buildings, Farm Yards and Rookeries——ah! Lord!——they're enough to ſtagnate the fineſt Flow of Spirits in the Univerſe.——*Bob,* you'll be at Lady *Everbloom*'s this Evening to drink Tea——

I know

know you'll be well entertain'd, becaufe you love Odi-
:s.

Briton, jun.

Her Ladyfhip did us the Honour to fend Cards this
[orning—who is to be there then ?

Dafh.

Why, very likely her Brother *Hardy*, the Bluff *Eaft*
dia Captain, whóm (as fhe is circumftanced) poor Devil,
e dar'n't contradict in any of his Humours, which (by
e bye) are a little upon the diabolic fometimes.

Briton, jun.

O! I know the Captain; we meet frequently at *Lloyd's*;
e values himfelf greatly on his Staunchnefs to his King
nd Country; and to prove it, is for ever railing at the
olitics, Commerce, Manners and Cuftoms of the *French*
[ation.

Dafh.

You have him to a Hair. Then there'll be Mifs *Barbara*
anguifh, the Creole from *Barbadoes*, an immenfe Fortune;
fine Snap for you, young *Cornwall*, I can tell you, if you
in but whifper a few foft things in her Ear — Have you
1y Blood in you?

Letty.

That's the very Lady my Brother was recommending
ft Night; I'm oblig'd to him.　　　　　　　[*Afide.*

Har.

Harriot.

I don't want Spirit, Sir, upon proper Occasions.

Dash.

Well said, my Buck————nay, the Devil a Danger in the Attack; you have nothing to do but load and fire— she's her own Governess; and, by what I can judge of her Discipline, if she keeps the Fortress five Days after your first Cannonade, I shall be damnably out in my Guess ————But 'tis the City of *London* to a pickled Cucumber she surrenders in less than a Fortnight.

Letty.

How comes it about, Sir, that you reject so valuable, and, at the same time, so easy a Capture yourself, pray?

Dash.

Why my dear little cherry Cheeks, I'll tell you; it is be- cause I have no less than four Women of tip-top Rank now under Bombardment, besides two others so closely besieged by Brigadier *Ballen O Mona*, that I must, in Honour, fly to their Relief; and what Skirmishes may happen upon the March, you know, are altogether uncertain—Yes, yes, *Prussia* and I have our Hands full.————

Letty.

Impudent! vain Fool!   {*Aside.*

Dash.

Dash.

Then we shall have Miss *Bellmont* ; O! a sweet Wench, and the most exquisite Singer! ah !—all your Thrushes, Goldfinches, Woodlarks and Nightingales, are no more to compare to her, my little Queen of the Meadows, than a Screech Owl is to a *Canary* Bird, or a Crab to a Pippin.

Briton, jun.

Will Lady Dowager *Layman* be there, Sir ?

Dash.

Lady *Layman*, O! fie! how cou'd you think of such an Indecency ? why she hasn't been out of her Apartment these four Days ; takes no manner of Diet, but Conserves and Jellies ; and sees no Soul living but the Priest ; have not you heard of her Loss ?—

Briton, jun.

Not I, truly.————What has it been, pray ?

Dash.

Then positively you amaze me !————I thought all the World had heard on't.————Her favourite rough Lapdog, *Jock,* that Father *Kelley* brought her from *Naples*—

Briton, jun.

May one depend upon this ?————you'll excuse me ; but really there is so much false Intelligence propagated, one doesn't know whom to credit.

Dash.

(256)

Dash.

A Fact; upon my Honour!—choak'd himself laft *Saturday* Morning at Supper, with the Wing of an Ortolan.

Briton, jun.

And the poor Lady's inconfolable!

Dash.

Upon the Margin of Madnefs.—Then we fhall have Mrs. *Potiphar* from *Duke's-place*; a Woman of no great Entertainment, but as fhe always vifits with her Purfe full of Money——is immoderately fond of Play, knows nothing of the Matter, and never wrangles; bearable enough.

Briton jun.

My Lady expects a great deal of Company——

Dash.

O, yes! Coming down *Pall Mall* juft now, who d'ye think pop't upon me out of Sir *Marmaduke Funlove's?* only 'Squire *Sam*, as gay as a Gambler upon a good Run; or a *French* Milliner on the fifth Sale of her veftal Incumbrance————ha, ha, ha.

Briton, jun.

Sam Hand!————I thought he had not been in Town; I haven't fee him at *George's* lately.————

Dash.

Dash.

May be he came laſt Night ;——ſo I made him promiſe to be there too, and to bring his Friend *Outré,* the
Mimic, with him ; he tells me he has pick'd up ſome
excellent new Characters——*Sam*'s a good natur'd Fellow, but ſuch a maggotty Dog there's no great Dependence upon him. [*Pulls out his Watch.*] Odſo ! I muſt
run up to Doctor *Gimcrack*'s, or I ſhall be too late for the
Sale.

Briton jun.

Of what, pray ?

Dash.

The beſt private Collection of Pictures, Shells, Prints,
Butterflies, and other Foſcets, perhaps, in *Europe*, that
the Reverend deceaſed had been making with great Study
and Pains for theſe forty Years——Well, your Servant.
                                                    [*Going.*

Briton jun.

Sir, I am your moſt Obedient——

Dash.

[*Returning.*] Ha, ha, ha, I had forgot one thing——
I muſt make you laugh !——do you know that that ſtupid Dolt of a Fellow, *Parſon Slubber-Text* has had the Aſ-
ſurance to ſend a Card to *Lady Dorothy Dawdle,* to inform
her that if ſhe does not put off her *Sunday* Night's Card-
playing, he ſhall exclaim againſt her from the Pulpit :
only think o'that ; did you ever hear any thing to come
up to't ?

S   *Eriton*

Briton jun.

Very impudent, indeed!

Dash.

Imprudent, say you! scandalous! wicked!————but Lady *Dolly's* Hand and Glove, with his Patron, Lord *Worthless*; the Fellow didn't know a Word o'that, I suppose: ah! a little Stripping and Starving will be absolutely necessary for the Doctor upon this Occasion;———— a blessed Time on't, indeed, we should have, if People of Quality's—— Amusements were to be curtail'd and interrupted at every officious Puppy's Pleasure, that had a Mind to set up for the Reformation of Manners———— Ha, ha, ha,————well————*au Revoir*————your Servant.   [*Exit Dash, singing.*

Harriet.

What an insignificant rattling Puppy 'tis.

Briton jun.

The Town swarms with 'em————

Harriet.

But I wonder, Sir, that you, who are so much the Reverse in your own Disposition, can bear the Mixture of such Reptiles among your Acquaintance?

Briton

Briton jun.

It is impoffible to avoid it, unlefs you were refolv'd to turn Hermit at once, fequefter yourfelf in fome obfcure Nook, and live at open War with Society.

Harriot.

But I fhou'd think now, that ferious Admonitions from Men of your Underftanding, might go a great Way towards the Reformation of fuch fuperficial Creatures ; and if there are any amongft 'em poffeft of fome fhining Qualities, it would be Charity in you to endeavour to remove the Clouds that interpofe, and prevent the World the Benefit of their Luftre.

Briton jun.

There is no pretending to correct Errors, without firft bringing your Pupil to be fenfible that they are fo ; and that we may fet down as a more than *Augean* Tafk, with regard to a Coxcomb ; fince the beft Authors have hitherto proved it an unfurmountable one——A Coxcomb is a Being compos'd from every thing contemptible, and yet fo well fatisfied, that, deaf to Confcience, Cenfure, or Precept, he continually runs counter to Reafon, and has no one thing to value himfelf upon, but what every body defpifes.

Enter

Enter a Servant.

Servant.

Sir, my Master is just come in, and Dinner is ready to be served up.

Briton jun.

Very well——Come, Sir.

[*Leads his Sister off.*
Exeunt.

Scene changes.

Miss Pen *and Miss* Dolly *meeting.*

Dolly.

Well, Miss *Pen,* how do you like this young Gentleman, our new Lodger?

Pen.

I don't know; I like him well enough.　　[*Carelessly.*

Dolly.

Well enough! is that all? why—ar'n't you in love with him?

Pen.

In Love with him! for what?—— not I indeed: I could venture through an Army of Twenty Thousand

such

such pretty Masters as he, and bring my Heart safe to its Quarters——No, no; the God must rumage his Quiver afresh; this Arrow hath no Point for me, I promise you.

Dolly.

You are a strange mad Girl: But what Objections can you have to him?

Pen.

Many, many, my Dear, many; but the main is that I think he looks too much like one of us. My Man now (if ever I should be entrusted with a Man) must be of a quite different Structure. I abominate your Shiverers at the Morning-Air, as the Song calls them.

Dolly.

That he has a good Complexion, I grant you; and a soft Manner of Expression: But his Deportment is far from effeminate, and——

Pen.

Well! I don't admire him.

Dolly.

That may arise from his not admiring you, perhaps.

Pen.

Pen.

Oh, dear Miss! ——why I am neither old, deformed, nor ugly——and why not admire me, pray? He has n't told you any thing to the contrary, I suppose: —— You are not so familiar together yet, are you?

Dolly.

Not I, indeed; but there is some little Judgment, you know, to be made from Eyes: I observed no Glances fly towards your Part of the Counter.

Enter Mrs. Spruce.

Mrs. Spruce.

Come, come, Girls, pray get to work; you know Lady *Squeamish* expects her Childbed-linen home To-morrow; and People of her Quality are seldom certain themselves at what Time they may have Occasion for't. ——And then there's Captain *O'Revory* mus'n't by any Means be disappointed; for if he misses the Brewer's widow, I may whoop for my Money, I'm sure o' that.—— What is it you have been chattering about, prithee?

Dolly.

Why, Madam, Miss *Pen* won't allow Mr. *Bellmour* handsome, and so we have been disputing about it,—— that's all.

Mrs.

Mrs. Spruce.

Oh fie upon't! fie upon't! —— I think such young Girls as you might find themselves something else to talk of. —— I'm asham'd of ye, absolutely ashamed of ye.

Dolly.

Lard, Ma'am, is there any Harm in saying that one thinks a Person handsome?

Mrs. Spruce.

Yes, Miss, a great deal of Harm.——When I was at your Age I have heard my Mama say, it was very impudent to look a Man in the Face long enough to know whether he was handsome or ugly. ——Go, go into the Shop, and mind your Business   *Exit.*

Miss Pen.

I don't know how ignorant of Mankind your Mama might keep you whilst you was under her Care, but you're vastly improved in the Study since, or I'm much out of my Judgment.   *Exeunt.*

ACT

ACT II.

A Side-board—A Servant attending at it—Desert upon the Table as after Dinner.

Lady Everbloom, *Miss* Languish, *Miss* Bellmont, Briton *jun.* Eetty, Harriot, Dash, *and others, walking about.*

Lady Everbloom.

'Have you seen an Opera yet, 'Sir? [*To Harriot.*]

Harriot.

No, an please your Ladyship.

Lady Everbloom.

No! ——I'm aftonish'd! What in *London* near three Weeks and not feen an Opera!

Harriot.

I am not fond of Mr. *Briton's* Character of 'em, Madam; he feems to think 'em but an infipid kind of Entertainment at beft, and they muft be particularly fo to me, who underftand not *Italian*.

Daſh.

Italian ! —— You have Eyes and Ears, my dear *Bel-*
lmour : You can underſtand that there are Angels in the
Boxes, Harmony to its higheſt Pitch in the Orcheſtra,
and ten Thouſand Tranſports in every thrilling Note of
the divine *Mattei !* Oh ! I doat upon Operas !——Don't
you, Miſs *Languiſh ?*

Miſs Languiſh.

No, Sir, upon my Word, nor can I help thinking
with this Gentleman, that neither Benefit or Pleaſure can
poſſibly be reap'd from any Maſter one's at a Loſs for the
Senſe of.

Daſh.

My Stars !——Here's a Rout about Senſe, indeed !—
Give me a good-humour'd, whimſical, outré, rattling kind
of a Blood now, that runs about here and there, and ſees and
hears all that is to be ſeen and heard, but never troubles
his Head about Reaſons or Conſequences at all ; who
has always a droll Story ready, no matter at whoſe Ex-
pence, or whether it be true or falſe, ſo it diverts his
Acquaintance ; this is the Man for me. Damn your
Hum-drums : People of great Senſe and Underſtanding,
(as they are call'd) are the moſt ſtupid, gloomy Beings
under the Sun to me.—

Briton jun.

I remember to have ſeen you at *Sheridan's* Lectures, as
well as at *King's* and *Demainbray's* ; and I have often heard
you ſay that you never miſs a Performance of Mr.
Garrick ; now if the hopes of being ſeriouſly and well

entertain'd, carries you not to thofe Places, I fhould be glad to know what it is that does.

Daſh.

Vogue, vogue, my Dear, vogue; the ſelf-ſame Thing that carries Lady *Sprightly* to Church, and Baron *Bubble* to Auctions; though all the World knows that the one haſn't a ſingle Grain of Religion, nor the other an Atom of Judgment.—Ha, ha, ha!

Lady Everbloom.

Pray, Mr. *Daſh*, (now you mention Auctions) who purchas'd that Piece of Painting that was put up juſt as I left the Room.

Daſh.

Does your Ladyſhip mean the Herd poſſeſs'd ——— by *Snider?*———

Lady Everbloom.

Yes.

Daſh.

It was knock'd down to Mr. *Ruben Iſachar* of *Hackney*, Madam, at one Hundred Guineas———He didn't much admire the Subject, I believe; but he ſaid it was ſo finely executed, he could not let it go by him.

[*A Craſh of breaking China within.*

Captain

Captain Hardy. [*Within*

You Rascal! you Villain!——come along, you sneaking Scoundrel.

Enter Captain Hardy, leading in a hearty looking Servant in one Hand, and with the other a French Valet ridiculously drest, &c.

Ha! ha! ha! Gentlemen and Ladies, I'm your humble Servant.——Here's a Contrast for you——ha! ha! ha!——Whoever this honest Fellow belongs to, I regard their Understanding: Downright *English* from Top to Toe, by the Lord——Which is your Master, Friend?

Servant.

That's my Lady, Sir.

Captain Hardy.

Why then I'm sure she's an *Antigallian* by her Choice of thee; and as such I respect her——Give me leave, Madam, to have a Smack at your lovely Lips, and to assure you that I honour your Judgment in this Man; 'tis sound and orthodox.——Here, my Son of Beef and Beer, here's a Crown for thee to drink the King's Health——and now you may go where your Duty calls you——but hear me!

Servant.

Servant.

Sir.

Captain Hardy.

Do you take good notice of this pimping, flimsy, gew-gaw, whip-sillabub Son of a Whore——this Disgrace to an honest Family——this Type of the magnanimous Enemies of *Great Britain*; and whenever you meet ~~this Fellow~~ him in your Walks, kick him; kick him, kick him lustily, for the Honour of a true-born *Englishman*, and the Good of your fellow Subjects.

Servant.

Shall I kick him now, Sir?

Captain Hardy.

No, not now——any other Time.

Servant.

Why then, Sir, I owe him a Crown's Worth; and I'll be now I die in his Debt.

Captain Hardy.

Right *English*——wants but a little setting too;——the best Fellows in the whole World; well commanded by the Lord *Harry* they are.

Lady

Lady Everbloom.

I was in hopes my Brother had been engaged for the Evening; he is in one of his Vagaries, I see; [*aside to Briton*] What is amiss now Sir, pray?

Captain Hardy.

Now, Sir? why the same that was then, Sir, and always will be, Sir——while you maintain such Vermin as these are in your House———Does'n't this Hound look like a fine Tutor for a young *Everbloom?*———a Fellow that's fit for no earthly Thing, except to disguise Faces, and turn whom Heaven design'd Men into Owls; ———or to supply the vacant Parts of an indispos'd Monkey, or air the Dogs in *Bloomsbury Fields.*

Lady Everbloom.

Pray, Brother, be quiet.

Captain Hardy.

I sha'nt be quiet; nor I won't let you be quiet, till I see you quit of your Trash.———I met the Fellow at the Door that runs about with his spaniel Puppies, white Blackbirds, Parroquets, Mocaws, and *Guiney* Hens; who, because he has no Nose himself, is for biting off every Body's else that has more Money than Wit; but I sent him packing. He has touch'd you for too much already ———That Rascal's Bills are like Bills of Honour, contracted without Thought, laden without Mercy, and paid without Delay; while those of an honest Tradesman may go to the Devil.

Lady

Lady Everbloom.

Fie, Brother, fie! I'm asham'd.

Captain Hardy.

And so you well may———— I tell you I'll have a Reformation in this Family; I'll weed it of its Rankness: And I'll begin with Monsieur here————Sirrah———— O you Dog!———— I wish Sir *Toby* was alive for your Sake, he'd reward you for teaching his Son to wash, patch, paint and perfume himself—Why, you Rascal, he'd skin you alive————Here, here, my Lady, here's your hopeful Son's whole Study now—here is his *Locke*, his *Boyle*, his *Euclid*, his *Newton*, his every Thing.

[Shewing a Bill of Articles.

Lady Everbloom.

Nay, but Brother————

Captain Hardy.

Nay, but Sister—hear your Son's curious Collection—do, 'tis worth while. [*Reads*] "The best Rouge from *Montpelier*—Lip-salve a la *Pompadour*—The royal beautifying Fluid—Eau de Luce, so much esteemed in *France*, that the Nobility never go without it in their Pockets—A most excellent Lotion for the speedy Removal of all Heats, Morphew, Pimples, &c."————I wish we had some Invention for the Removal of all Puppies and Coxcombs, with all my Heart.

[Looking at Dash.

Dash.

Dash.

Ah! that Stroke was levell'd at me now——It should not pass unanswer'd, but that he is such an infernal Brute there's no dealing, with any Degree of Decency, with him; for he pays no Regard at all to Wit; but upon the most insignificant Rub in the whole World talks of a great Stick and a Tilter—————Now as good Breeding will not permit me to carry the one, so a good Estate with good Discretion, prevents my making use of the other——No, no, he may play by himself for me, I am no Match for the Captain.

Captain Hardy.

These are part of the Stock in trade of my Nephew; the Lad that you have heard me say had a mind to go a Voyage with us to the *East Indies, Worthy*——he'd make a fine Sailor, to be sure, and be damn'd to him.

Lady Everbloom.

Do, Brother, have a little Patience in Regard of the Company.

Captain Hardy.

Faith I think I have shewn a very great Regard for you, and the Company too, to leave a banging Bowl brim full of Rack, and eight or nine of the jolliest Dogs in the Navy round it, to come to ye.

Dash.

I wish you were with your jolly Dogs again, with all my Heart, or any where else, so we were rid of you. [*Aside.*
Lady.

Lady Everbloom.

We are oblig'd to you, Brother, but why wou'dn't you bring your good Temper along with you?

Captain Hardy.

Temper! by the Lord-*Harry* I was in as good a Temper as any Man in the Kingdom could be, till I went into the Back-Parlour, and found your Son fitting there, wrapt up in a Sheet like *Margaret*'s Ghost, or a *Scotch* Whore doing Penance; and this *Dainty Davy* here tickling him up with his Pincers, Pencils, Puffs, and Brushes ——Damme if I knew the Lad, he was so transmogrified; however, seing me look musty, he cut and run, as we say, and very well for him that he did so, for when I was demolishing his Toilet (which I have done pretty effectually) 'tis Odds if he had 'scap'd without a few Marks of my Favour.

Dash.

To be sure he's vastly oblig'd to you.   [*Aside.*

Captain Hardy.

Here, Fellow!

[*The French Valet runs to him, he pushes him down.*

Not you, you Rascal!——Who waits?

Enter

Enter a Servant

Ay, why this Fellow looks like a Chriftian——Where's my Nephew?

Servant.

Gone out, Sir, ever fince you came in, almoft.

Captain Hardy.

Ay, I frighten'd him out of his Wits; I reckon we fhall fee him no more to Night—Well, it's no Matter—— Give me a Glafs of Wine—

Servant.

Wou'd your Honour pleafe to drink *Claret? Champagne? Burgundy? Frontiniac*———

Captain Hardy.

No, you Puppy, none of 'em—No; damn your Balderdafh, frothy as the Rafcals that make 'em———No, no, Give me a Bumper of found, honeft *Port*, and I'll drink a Health to the beft King in *Chriftendom.* ——— [*Servant gives Wine*] ——— King *George*'s Health, with all my Heart——Succefs to his Arms by Sea and Land, and may Confufion light upon all his Enemies —— [*Drinks*] —I'll tell you what, Sifter—Do but break your Son of being a Coxcomb, and we fhall never quarrel.

Lady

Lady Everbloom.

Nay, you shall have him entirely under your own Management, Captain, upon that Condition, and I dare say he will be conformable; for notwithstanding your Roughness at Times, he has a great Regard for you.

Captain Hardy.

Why, the Whelp has no other Reason, that I know of———You Scoundrel, come hither!

[To the Valet.

Valet.

Monsieur!   [*Comes cringing towards him*.

Captain Hardy.

Don't Mounseer me, you Puppy, don't Mounseer me ———Prithee what Place is it that you occupy in this Family?

Valet.

Je ne scai pas occupy—vat is you mean occupy, Sire? I no underftant occupy!———

Captain Hardy.

Why, what do you call yourself, Fool? what do you call yourself?

Valet.

Valet.

Mon-fire, I be ga Pardonne——en la Famille, en dis Famille, Sire; Je fuis, me ami Confiture, me makea de grande Sweeta-meats, et de fine riche Cordiels, pour ma chere Dame, my deard good Lady; et autretemps, me ami la Valet, a Monfieur, le young Squire.

Captain Hardy.

Why then, take this from me, that the young 'Squire fhall run no further Rifque of being made ten Times a greater Fool by you, than he has been by Nature; go you and tell him I fay fo: And that if he doefn't immediately change himfelf from the hobgoblin Figure I faw him cut juft now, pay you your Wages, and fend you packing, he has no further Pretenfions to my Favour.

Valet.

I fall takea de particular Care, Sive, to be fure; and I hope, Sire, your Honour, Capitaine, vil not hinder Monfieur, my Maitre, de leave to giva me one Charactere.

Captain Hardy.

A Character, ha!——Ay, that he fhall, and in two Words——A *Frenchman*——that's Character fufficient; you'll find Fools enough ready to receive you upon it— the more's the Pity——About your Bufinefs, go, turn it.

Dafh.

You are too hard upon the poor Fellow, Captain.

T 2

Captain

Captain Hardy.

Damn fuch poor Fellows——What are you one of their
Advocates, ah!—Ay, you look like fuch a one—I don't
know any Bufinefs they have here, efpecially at this
Time, unlefs it be to debauch us with Foppery, under-
mine us with Hypocrify, and over-run us with Popery
————But come, I thought we were to have had fome
of the Choice-Spirits here this Afternoon, and thrown
off afore now—Where's this *Sam Hand*, and the Fellow
that takes all the Players off, that you talk'd about?

Lady Everbloom.

We expect them, Brother, every Minute.

Captain Hardy.

Nay 'tisn't a Pin matter whether they come or not;
for I think there's no great Merit in encouraging a Mem-
ber of any Profeffion to ridicule and expofe the reft
————Why let's have a Song then——Here's *Jack
Worthy*, worthy *Jack*, as I call him, my Purfer, as merry,
as honeft, and as brave a Fellow as ever ftood true to
the Flag of *Great Britain*————None of your *Si vous plaife*,
none of your *Je vous remercie Men*————He fhall give
you one in turn, and he's no bad one I promife you.

Lady Everbloom.

Mifs *Bellmont*, will you grant us the Favour of the laft
new Ballad?

Mifs Bellmont.

With Pleafure, Madam.

Miſs Bellmont *ſings.*

I.

Nay urge me not, Hope, my fond Flame to reveal,
With an Angel's ſoft Face, her Heart's harder than Steel;
'Tis there that black Winter eternally reigns:
Love's Godhead ſhe ſcoffs at, his Temple diſdains.

II.

'Twere ſafer at Midnight thro' Deſarts to ſtray,
Where prowls the fierce Tyger in queſt of his Prey,
Than the Eyes of that Baſiliſk, *Sylvia,* abide;
Who ne'er look'd on Swain, but ſo ſurely he died.

III.

Sweet Boy, ever wont to make Mortals thy Care,
No longer the cruel'ſt of Tyrants forbear;
Thy beſt pointed Arrow—Oh! draw to the Head,
And pierce a proud Heart, for which Millions have bled.

Captain Hardy.

My little Bud of Beauty, I'm oblig'd to you
—— But to be plain with you, I don't like
your Song——I don't like it at any Rate; it's too fine
for me by a League: Damme, I hate your Hearts, and
Darts, and Swains, and Pains, and Loves, and Doves;
I'd rather hear the *American* War-whoop by half—No, no,
give me *The glorious Ninety-two,* or *Jolly* Bacchus *one Day
gaily ſtriding bis Ton*: They are the Songs for me——
Jack, my Boy, touch us off that that *Ralph Tier,* the

Boat-

Boatſwain made upon *Cherbourgh*——— Damme I like that
becauſe 'tis a good Subject, and a true Subject.

Purſer ſings.

I.

'Twas *Auguſt* the Seventh, at Three in the Morning,
  Our Cannon 'gainſt *Cherbourgh* began for to roar ;
Never ſtruck Colours, our Courage adorning,
  Grenadiers haſted away to the Shore.

Chorus.

Such is the Sport that *Britons* delight in;
Lead 'em well on, and they'll never fear fighting:

II.

'Midſt Fire and Smoke ſtood our bold Commodore,
  Balls flew around him———yet ne'er did he wince ;
Serene were his Orders on every Score,
  And cloſe by my Lord fought brave *Edward* the Prince.

Chorus.

Such is the Sport that *Britons* delight in ;
Lead 'em well on, and they'll never fear fighting.

III.

No more the *French* Monarch his *Cherbourgh* can boaſt,
  So hurtful to *England* for many a Year;
The Shipping all burnt, the Works ſhatter'd and toſt,
  And drove by Exploſion into the Air.

Chorus.

Such is the Sport that *Britons* delight in ;
Lead 'em well on, and they'll never fear fighting.

IV.

IV.

Some fay that our Prince was too gallantly bold,
   A Fault, we muft own, but a Fault we approve;
It runs in the Family, as I've been told,
   And that has fecur'd 'em *Great Britain*'s true Love:

Chorus.

Such is the Sport that *Britons* delight in;
Lead 'em well on, and they'll never fear fighting.

V.

Firm in the Praife of your worthy Commanders,
   Soldiers and Sailors, O make the Air ring;
Eaft or *Weft Indies*, *French* Coaft, or in *Flanders*,
   Revenge the brave *Dury*, and honour the King.

Chorus.

Such is the Sport that *Britons* delight in,
Lead 'em well on, and they'll never fear fighting.

Captain Hardy.

Well, what d'ye think of that now?

Lady Everbloom.

A moft excellent Song, indeed, Brother.

Mifs Languifh.

And charmingly fung.

Purfer.

Purser.

Your moſt obedient, Madam.

Captain Hardy.

And ſo it was, Miſs *Barbara*, and he's a good tight handſome Fellow too, isn't he?   Let me recommend him to you for a Huſband: Damme, he'll kiſs you out of your Senſes, and kiſs you into 'em again; he's worth a Thouſand of ſuch poor emaciated Mummies as *Obadiab* the Wine-merchant in *Mincing-Lane*. What ſay you? Can you fancy him?

Miſs Languiſh.

You are too haſty; Captain, too haſty by half.

Captain Hardy.

Not at all, Miſs *Barbara*——When young Folks ſeem to be made for one another, 'tis a Chriſtian-like Part to bring 'em together at once. 'Twou'd be a good Match; the Fellow's got Money. [*Aſide to her.*] *Jack*, I'd have you make up to her, I'll be damn'd if ſhe don't like you.   [*To him.*

Purser.

Do you think ſo, Sir?

Captain

Captain Hardy.

Think fo!—I know fo————Make Hay while the Sun
fhines, I tell you ; fhe won't ftay long for you : She
comes from a warm climate—She's none of your Chalk-
eaters—None of your Cynder-fcranchers. ———— Who is
that little fmirking Wench, do you know, *Briton ?*

[*Afide to Briton.*

Briton jun.

My Sifter, Sir.

Captain Hardy.

Your Sifter ! You don't tell me fo !

Briton jun.

Fact upon my Honour.

Captain Hardy.

Why, how long has fhe been in Town ?

Briton jun.

About three Weeks, Sir———— She came up with my
Father and that young Gentleman, a Neighbour of his.

Captain

Captain Hardy.

Why you furprife me!———my old Friend *Briton* in
Town three Weeks, and I know nothing of the Matter!
Why, Sir, your Father and I have, I warrant, drawn half
a Grofs of Corks together formerly : odfo, my old Friend
Jerry Briton in Town ; I'll go and pay my Refpects to him
directly———Where does he lodge?

Briton. jun.

In the fame Houfe with me : you have been there,
haven't you ?———

Captain Hardy.

Miftrefs *Spruce's* in the next Street ?—ay, ay, I know it.

Enter Servant.

Servant.

Every thing's ready in the Temple, Madam, as your
Ladyfhip order'd.———

Lady Everbloom.

Very well ; we'll play at Cards there then ; 'tis cool and
pleafant ; we are all for the Play, Brother, to-night, and
thence to Lady *Brag's* Route ;—I fuppofe we muft expect
you for one of the Party.

Captain Hardy.

Not I, faith ; I wou'dn't defer myfelf the Pleafure of
taking an old Friend by the Fift for all the Plays in the
Uni-

Univerfe: but I'd have you go, *Jack*; you're a Woman's
Man [*To Purfer*] and as to Routes, I abominate all Routes
but a *French* Route. If a Body now could fee twenty
thoufand brave refolute *English*, Sword in Hand, at the
Heels of treble the Number of run-away *French*; that
wou'd be a Route, fomething like a Route, a Route worth
the Talking of.———Well—I wifh you well diverted—
Gentlemen and Ladies your Servant.—

All.

Your Servant, Sir.   [*Exit Captain Hardy.*

Dafh.

Your moft obedient Servant, Sir———I wifh you was
juft now doubling the *Cape*, with all my Heart—I wonder
how your Ladyfhip does to bear with the Captain, for you
are the very Quinteffence of good Breeding yourfelf, and
he's as indelicate as a *Hottentot*.———Will your Ladyfhip
do me the Honour———

[*Exeunt*, Dafh *leading Lady* Everbloom.

SCENE *changes to Mr.* Briton's *Apartment.*

Enter Harriot *and* Letty.

Harriot.

If you have any Confideration yet left for yourfelf, or
me, abate this Violence of Temper; how can you urge
me thus with Reproaches you cannot but be fenfible are
unjuft and groundlefs.———

Letty.

Letty.

Wou'd I were not too senfible of the Reverfe; I am neither deaf nor blind, Sir, whatever you may imagine me; and furely I muft have been both, not to have ob-ferved your very particular Behaviour with Mifs *Languifh*, a Creature that has nothing in the World to recommend her, except Money.

Harriot.

Mifs *Languifh* !

Letty.

I faid, Sir, Mifs *Languifh*; and though my Brother and you have taken fuch mighty Pains to conceal the Matter, I am not at a Lofs for Intelligence; it is no Secret to me that it has been, by his Advice, you addrefs her; and that from his Introduction and Sollicitation in your Favour you are to expect your Encouragement.

Harriot.

That I have fome Expectations from your Brother's Af-fection for me, I confefs; tho' not of the Kind your ridi-culous Jealoufy prompts you to fancy, I affure you——hufh——your Father——

Enter Briton *fen.* Briton *jun. and Captain* Hardy.

Briton fen.

Your Servant, Mr. *Bellmour*, how does my Girl? Your Brother tells me you have been indifpos'd, which brought you Home earlier than you expected.

Letty.

Letty.

We had a great deal of Company at my Lady's————
The Heat of the Room overpower'd me a little, and occafion'd a flight Head-ach, but 'tis gone off————I thank
you, Sir.

Briton, fen.

That's well————

Harriot.

I am not forry it happen'd now, as it furnifh'd us with
a good Excufe to come Home, without being lugg'd to
the Route; which, as I never play, would have afforded
me but dull Entertainment.

Captain Hardy.

Never game, Sir, do you?

Harriot.

Never had the leaft Propenfity to it, Captain?

Captain Hardy.

I am glad of it, Sir, and I wifh all the young Fellows in
England were of your Opinion, with all my Heart. A
Pox on't————it's a curs'd Itch, a curs'd Itch indeed!——
an Itch, Sir, that has been the Ruin of many a fine Gentleman; and, (by the bye) many a fine Lady too, to my
Knowledge————I am amaz'd People of any Share of
Underftanding will give into't; for it is certainly the
moft abfurd, and moft defencelefs of all human Extrava-
gancies.

Enter

Enter Servant.

Servant.

A Letter, Sir——— [*To B iton,* fen.

Briton, fen.

From Sir *Aston,* Sir, [*To Harriot*] —with your Leave,
Captain—you are all Friends—

Captain Hardy.

No Apology, good Sir———

Briton fen. *reads.*

Friend Briton,

" Your Scruples are honourable, but needlefs, on ac-
" count of an Error incumbent on me to clear; a youth-
" ful Connection occafion'd an Agreement between a
" Friend and I never to marry; the Survivor to become
" the other's fole Executor; Affection for my late Lady
" made me propofe difannulling the Contract; he con-
" fented, but declared it ftill binding with him whilft he
" continued fingle. A few Months afterwards a violent
" Fever carried him off, and indeed left me worth all
" he died poffefs'd of. At my Deceafe, however, (if
" without Male Iffue) the Whole to defcend to a Ne-
" phew, his only Relation, who likewife dying a Batche-
" lor, the fuppos'd Youth, now under your Care, whom,
" as we never had a Son, we thought it neceffary to im-
" pofe on the World as fuch, became, not Heir indeed,
" but Heirefs to one of the fineft Eftates in the Weft; it
" is

" is fit the Amour fhou'd be drop'd between *Afton Bell_*
" *mour* and your Daughter; but if any Engagement fhall
" be propofed to *Harriot Bellmour*, that her Prudence di-
" rects her to accept, her Will is her own, and I fhall
" be ready to ratify it.".

Afton Bellmour.

Harriot.

All Matter of Fact! I plead guilty; and thereupon
freely relinquifh the Title of *Afton Bellmour*, Efq; for that
of *Harriot Bellmour*, Spinfter, and fubmit myfelf to the
Mercy of the Court.————

Captain Hardy.

Egad, a fine Wench!—a fine Wench indeed! upon my
Soul a fine Wench!—fine Face, fine Limbs—fine—but
how in the Name of Wonder—.

Harriot.

You have heard the Reafons affign'd for my early Difguife as a Boy; and as fuch I have been bred and edu-
cated; and though there has been no Danger in the Dif-
covery for thefe two Years paft, yet it had ftill remain'd
a Secret, had not the frequently repeated Eulogiums on
your Character, Sir, from both our Fathers, excited my
Curiofity to become a nearer Witnefs of Deferts, which I
am now convinced their Praifes were fcarcely adequate to.

Briton jun.

You over-rate my poor Endeavours to merit your
Efteem. Permit me, Madam, however, to affure you,
on my Credit, that from the firft Sight of you, a fecret
Impulfe actuated upon my Heart, with a Degree of
Fond-

Fondnefs beyond Defcription; a Tendernefs unfelt, un-
known, till then; fomething above the Friendfhip due
from Man to Man, tho' at that time not to be accounted
for.

Harriot.

Then I fhall indeed be happy!————for after what I
have already faid, nothing remains more for me to fay,
but that I pride myfelf in the avowing an honourable
Paffion for a meritorious Object; and here diveft myfelf
of that over-fcrupulous (and too often affected) Referve
of my Sex, whilft I affure Mr. *Briton*, that my Perfon and
Fortune, fuch as they are, if they may be deem'd agreeable to him, are entirely at his Acceptance.

Briton jun.

Agreeable!————O! my Soul! fhall I ever be able,
with all the Gratitude I am Mafter of, to convince yo
how much I efteem the Bleffing?————Fortune, I thank
thee! O! thou haft caft a Jewel in my Way, long, long
fearch'd in Vain————a Woman truly valuable.

Harriot.

[*To Letty.*] Come, cheer up, my Dear:————I might
have undeceiv'd you fooner, but I was willing to make
fure of my Mark————tho' I can't marry you, I fhan't go
out of the Family you fee. As Sifters we may agree perhaps better than as Hufband and Wife.

Captain Hardy.

Let who will doubt that————for I am fure I don't.
————She muft needs make you a very good Wife,
Briton,

Briton—for she's damn'd tir'd of wearing the Breeches, I see that.

Harriot.

In some Degree to make Amends for my long Abuse of your Credulity, I shall (with your Brother's Leave, to whom all I have now belongs) add so considerably to your Fortune, as, with your own natural Perfections, cannot fail to procure you a good Husband.—Upon this Condition, that you upbraid me no more with Miss *Languish* tho'.   [*Smiling.*

Briton jun.

My Leave!———Generous Creature!———I have no Leave———no Will———no Wish but your's——— your Pleasure shall always constitute my Happiness.

Briton sen.

A Change of Affairs so sudden, who cou'd have suspected—— but Providence orders all things for the best. My Children, I give you my Blessing, and wish you all the Joy and Happiness your Qualifications merit.

Captain Hardy.

Why that's as it shou'd be, now; but d'ye hear; we must not let this poor Wench be disappointed neither. Why, my old Friend, you'll have your Sheets gnaw'd to Pieces; you won't have a whole Pair in your Stock shortly: we must look out for a Husband for her, by the Lord *Harry*, we must, we must, efaith!

Letty.

I am oblig'd to you, Sir, but you may spare yourself that Trouble; having been so very unsuccessful on my first setting out in the Road of Matrimony, I believe I shall lay aside all future Thoughts of the Journey.

Captain Hardy.

And turn Nun, I suppose, ha!———no, no, not you, indeed; we'll find you better Employment; your Father is too honest a Man to encourage Popish Ceremonies; his House shall be no Convent. How think you of my Nephew? he's a sprightly Lad; how think you of *Jack?*

Harriot.

To deal freely with you, Captain,—I know, most contemptibly———

Captain Hardy.

Does she indeed? hum!———I like her the better for't———for he's as damn'd a Puppy as any in *England,* that's certain. Cou'd you fancy me, Miss?

Letty.

You, Sir!

Captain Hardy.

Ay, me, my Dear! why I'm not joking you———think on't a bit———You may be worse offer'd.———I like your Daughter well, Friend *Briton;* she isn't like our Town Women a bit; no, no, there's good wholesome
Flesh

Flesh and Blood; she's none of your Fashion-mongers neither, I see; none of your *French* Gewgaws about her; I like her for that.

Briton sen.

Are you serious, Captain, tho'?

Captain Hardy.

Ay, by the Lord am I; and to prove it I'll go along with you down to *Newgrove*; who knows what a Month's better Acquaintance may bring about.

Briton sen.

Her Spirits are a good deal chagrin'd at present, Captain, but when a little Time and Reflection have worn that off, if you are really in earnest upon the Affair, you'll meet with a grateful Acknowledgment on her Part, I make no Doubt. She's a very good Girl; but of that at a more convenient Opportunity.

Captain Hardy.

I'll tell you what I propose, and that is to see *Bob* and *Harriot* here, made as happy as the Parson can make 'em to-morrow Morning; that Sir *Afton* shall have an Account of it transmitted to him to-morrow Evening; and that we all set out in a Party together for *Newgrove* to-morrow Fortnight.

Briton jun.

An excellent Proposal, Captain; what says my *Harriot* to it?

Captain

Captain Hardy.

Pſhaw! ſhe has nothing to ſay againſt it, I am ſure; and it ſhall be ſo; and we'll have a jolly Day, and a jolly Night; and ah, my old Friend, you and I have ſat Foot to Foot e're now, and crack'd half a Dozen Bottles of good old Port together; han't we Boy!

Briton ſen.

Ay, ſure, and may again, Sir.

Captain Hardy.

May again, Sir! ay, and again and again, Sir; and who's to hinder us? And to-morrow Night, Sir, after we have put the young Folks to Bed, we'll have one thorough Soaking till we are as red, and as greaſy as a Brace of mendicant Fryars, juſt come from regaling their Noſes at the charitable Expences of the miſerable Bigots that harbour them.

Briton ſen.

I am glad to ſee you ſo merry, Captain——

Captain Hardy.

Damn it, I'm always ſo; there's nothing like it, Maſter *Briton*; who can be ſad, and live in *England?* none, but damn'd ſad Fellows indeed——We have Peace and Plenty at Home at leaſt, let things go how they will Abroad; and good Laws, and Liberties, and Properties well protected; and what Reaſon have *Engliſhmen* to be ſad, I

want

want to know then—Well! what says your Lady to my Proposal for to-morrow? [*To* Briton *jun.*

Harriot.

For my Part I am now under Mr. *Briton*'s Conduct, Sir; he is to do as he thinks proper; it is my Duty to be conformable.

Briton jun.

My sweet obliging Girl—why then, Sir, be it as you say—and now—nothing shall part us whilst Heaven continues our Lives. [*Takes her Hand.*

The Cement good, and the Foundation sure,
Such Edifice must doubtless long endure.
Let us then hope, since Virtue, Health and Youth,
Compose the Cement, and we build on Truth.

U 3

A SONG.

Sung this Seafon at *Sadler's Wells*, by Mr. *Andrews.*

I.

FROM the Projects fo vain,
    Of *France* or of *Spain*,
Britannia's brave Sons fhall defend her:
    I'm a Proteftant born,
    And of confequence fcorn
The Devil, the Pope, and Pretender.
A Pox o'their Friars, Books, Candles, and Bells,
Their Bulls, Abfolutions, their Saints, and their Cells.

II.

    We're furely undone,
    If once over-run
By Priefts, Papifts, *Rome*, and ftarv'd Bullies,
    Who never yet eat
    An Ounce of good Meat,
Or know what a Belly brim-full is.
Our Grounds with the Locufts wou'd foon be o'erfpread,
Our felves, Wives, and Children be knock'd on the Head.

III.

III.

For Corn-fields fo rich,
  Poor Dogs, how they itch;
A Bleffing they ne'er fhall obtain :
  Good Hearts and great Guns
  Tell run-away Dons
We will not be brow-beat by *Spain*;
He muft be a Wretch who refufes to fight
For Religion, for Freedom, his King, and his Right.

IV.

By the Pope and his Tools,
  The great Bugbears of Fools,
Falfe Whims they've been led to purfue;
  Whilft the *Britifh* Defigns
  Shall be paid by the Mines
Of *Chili, Potofi, Peru :*
The proud Priefts fhall be ftript of their ill-gotten Gain,
And our Tars return greater than Grandees of *Spain*.

The

The M I S T A K E.

Sung this Season at *Sadler's Wells* by Mr. *Andrews.*

I.

ON *Tuesday,* the fourth of sweet *May,*
    I first met young *Sophy* the clever;
Thought I, cou'd I wed but a Nymph half so
    gay,
    I sure shou'd be happy for ever.

II.

I watch'd the 'Fair home, and on *Wednesday* addrest,
    I found her quite pleasant and clever;
A Passion for me she as frankly exprefs'd;
    I thought myself happy for ever.

III.

On *Thursday* I ask'd of her Aunt her Consent,
    She gave it free, easy and clever;
I thought I indeed had too much of Content,
    And sure to be happy for ever.

IV.

IV.

On *Friday* all day thro' the City we drove,
    To lay in the Properties clever ;
Silks, Ribbands, and Lace, as the Proofs of my Love;
    I thought myfelf happy for ever.

V.

The Ring and the Licenfe on *Saturday* bought,
    And all Things made ready and clever,
To change with a Duke I'd not given a Groat ;
    I thought myfelf happy for ever.

VI.

As pert as a Monkey, and as gay as a Lark,
    On *Sunday* I dreft me full clever ;
Sure never was half fo conceited a Spark,
    I thought myfelf happy for ever.

VII.

But e're we had paft than a month little more,
    Things alter'd that late were fo clever ;
In Debt upon Debt I was plung'd o'er and o'er,
    And found myfelf ruin'd for ever.

F I N I S.

CONTENTS.

Epi-

CONTENTS.

A

CONTENTS.

A

CONTENTS.

On

CONTENTS.

Lightning Source UK Ltd.
Milton Keynes UK
UKHW052235250123
415916UK00022B/94